From Verse to Voice

Letting the Word Do the Work

(A Simple Guide to Writing Devotions Without Overthinking It)

Kimberly Billings

**FAVOR DEI
PRESS**
NEW YORK

From Verse to Voice
Letting the Word Do the Work
(A Simple Guide to Writing Devotions Without Overthinking It)

First Edition
Copyright © 2026 Favor Dei Press
All rights reserved.

Cover Designer: Kimberly Billings

ISBN: 979-8-9993690-2-4
Printed in United States of America

TABLE OF CONTENTS

INTRODUCTION

- You Don't Have to Be a Writer
- Why This Book Exists
- Devotional Writing Isn't Elite
- God Speaks First
- We Respond
- How to Use This Book (Alone or in a Group)

PART I: WHY THIS MATTERS

1. God Speaks First

- The Word Does the Work
- We Are Responders, Not Initiators
- Grace Before Effort
- Pause Here
- Try This

2. What Is a Devotion (And What It Isn't)?

- Not a Sermon
- Not a Diary Entry
- Not a Theology Paper
- Reflection Rooted in Scripture
- Pause Here
- Try This

- Then Personal Connection
- Staying Grounded in the Text
- Avoiding Drift
- Practice Section

7. Asking Questions That Actually Help

- Weak vs. Strong Questions
- Gentle Invitations vs. Guilt
- Law/Gospel Balance
- If Questions Aren't Your Thing
- Practice Section

8. Writing an Honest Prayer

- Keep It Simple
- Avoid Performance
- When You Don't Know What to Sa
- Different Tones of Prayer
- Fill-in-the-Blank Templates
- Practice Section

9. Crafting the One-Liner

- Why It Matters
- Clear Over Clever
- Not Cheesy
- Truth in One Sentence
- Practice Section

PART III: WRITING WITH DEPTH

10. Fully Worked Sample Devotions

- Comfort
- Identity
- Repentance
- Calling
- Hope
- Doubt
- Waiting
- Ordinary Faithfulness

11. Common Devotional Writing Mistakes

- Turning Every Verse into "Try Harder"
- Turning Every Story Into "Be More Like Them"
- Forgetting the Cross
- Making Grace Too Small
- Saying Things That Sound Biblical but Aren't
- When Devotion Turns into Self-Help
- When We Try to Sound Too Deep
- Keep Order Clear
- A Gentle Check
- Why This Matters

12. When You Feel Like a Fraud

- "Who Am I to Write This?"
- Writing While Still Being Shaped
- Writing When You Don't Feel It
- Dry seasons
- The Pressure to Sound Deep

Introduction

Let's get this out of the way first: you don't have to be a writer.

You don't have to be a published author.

You don't have to be a theologian.

You don't have to be eloquent, poetic, deep, or what someone might call "the devotional type."

You need a Bible and a willing heart.

That's it.

For a long time, I assumed devotional writing belonged to other people. The super-spiritual ones. The perfectly articulate ones. The ones who journal in color-coded pens and draw beautiful lettering in the margins of their Bibles. I assumed it required a certain personality, a certain depth, or a certain kind of spiritual polish.

It does not.

I realized this slowly.

I would sit with a group — sometimes teens, sometimes adults — and ask a simple question: "What is God saying in this verse?"

The reaction was almost always the same.

Silence.

Not because they didn't love Scripture. Not because they didn't believe it. But because they suddenly felt responsible for saying something impressive.

That pressure is heavy.

Some would shrug. Some would look down. Some would say, "I don't know... I'm not good at this stuff." And I remember thinking, this is not supposed to feel like a performance.

Devotional writing is simply responding to what God has already said.

It's not about impressing anyone.

It's about listening.

It's about slowing down long enough to let a single verse press into real life.

If you've ever underlined a sentence and thought, "Ooh, that one stung," or whispered, "That is exactly what I needed," you are already doing the heart work of devotional writing. Putting it into words is simply the next step.

God Speaks First

Before going any further, something important needs to be clear: God speaks first.

Scripture isn't waiting for your creativity to make it meaningful. It's already living and active. Hebrews 4:12 tells us that "the Word of God is living and active, sharper than any two-edged sword." That means it cuts before we ever comment on it. It exposes before we ever explain it. It comforts before we ever summarize it.

The Holy Spirit works through the Word — not through our cleverness.

That matters.

When you open your Bible, you are not stepping into a brainstorming session. You are stepping into something already alive. God is speaking. The Spirit is working. You are not the initiator. You are the responder.

That changes the pressure.

You are not here to manufacture insight.

You are here to notice what is already happening.

Sometimes the Word exposes what needs repentance. Sometimes it delivers comfort that feels almost too personal to explain. Often it does both at the same time.

The Law shows us our need.

The Gospel shows us Christ.

Devotional writing does not add power to Scripture. It simply gives you space to acknowledge what that power is already doing.

Writing a devotion doesn't earn you favor with God. It doesn't make you more spiritual. It doesn't upgrade your standing.

It is a practice of attention.

Attention to the Word.

Attention to your own heart.

Attention to the quiet way the Spirit convicts, comforts, steadies, and redirects.

You're not performing.

You're receiving and then responding.

Why Writing Changes How You Listen

There's something about writing that slows you down.

You can read quickly.

You can skim.

You can nod along.

Writing forces you to stay.

When you try to put a verse into your own words, you suddenly notice what you had been skipping. You realize when you don't actually understand something. You see where your assumptions filled in gaps.

Writing exposes drift.

It also reveals grace.

Sometimes you think you understand a verse — until you try to explain it. Then you realize how much more is there. Other times, a verse you've read a hundred times suddenly feels new because you sat with it long enough to let it breathe.

This book is not about producing something polished. It's about practicing attention in a way that reshapes how you hear.

When you move from verse to voice, you're not creating meaning. You're articulating what you're receiving.

And articulation deepens formation.

What This Book Is (And What It Isn't)

Let's clear a few things up.

This book is not:

• A theology textbook

• A preaching manual

• A Bible study curriculum with answer keys

• A journaling exercise disconnected from Scripture

• A platform-building guide for devotional influencers

This is not about crafting something that sounds devotional.

It is about learning how to respond to Scripture faithfully and honestly.

This book is:

• A workshop in written form

• A simple structure you can repeat

• A steady rhythm you can return to

• A practice space

Nothing fancy.

Nothing performative.

Nothing complicated.

Just a clear pattern:

Begin with the verse.

Reflect on what it says.

Include a question if it helps you think more deeply.

Write a simple prayer.

Capture one clear takeaway.

That's it.

Full stop.

Who This Is For

This guide is for the person who has never written a devotion before.

It's for the new believer who loves Scripture but feels unsure how to respond to it.

It's for the lifelong Christian who has read the Bible for decades but never put reflection into words.

It's for teens who want something practical and real.

It's for adults who want something structured.

It works for individuals sitting alone at a kitchen table.

It works for small groups gathered around folding chairs.

There is no grading scale here.

No gold stars.

No performance review.

There is simply practice.

Practice listening carefully.

Practice responding honestly.

Practice trusting that the Word does the real work.

A Roadmap for Where We're Going

Part I grounds us in why this matters.

We'll talk about what a devotion is (and isn't), how Law and Gospel shape reflection, and why your real voice matters more than spiritual polish.

Part II builds the structure.

You'll learn how to choose a verse without overthinking it, write a reflection that stays anchored in the text, ask helpful questions, pray honestly, and craft a clear one-liner.

Part III is practice.

You'll see full examples, work through templates, and take on a simple 30-day challenge to build consistency.

By the end, you won't just understand devotional writing.

You'll be doing it.

You don't have to sound profound.

You don't have to uncover hidden meaning in every verse.

You open the Word.

You read it carefully.

You notice what it's doing.

You respond honestly.

The power rests in the One who speaks.

This is where we begin.

Ready?

Grab your Bible or open your favorite Bible app. Find that favorite pen — you know the one.

Let's do this.

Heavenly Father, bless the reader of this book. Work through Your Holy Spirit to guide their thoughts, their understanding, and their words as they reflect on Your Holy Word. In Jesus' name, Amen.

PART I: WHY THIS MATTERS

Chapter 1

God Speaks First

There was a season when I opened my Bible already thinking about what I might write.

I didn't recognize it at first. It looked spiritual enough — Bible open, notebook ready, pen in hand. It felt disciplined. But underneath that setup was a quiet pressure: I needed to come away with something good. Something thoughtful. Something that sounded like it belonged in a devotional book.

That subtle shift changes everything.

Instead of reading to hear what God is saying, you begin reading to find material. The verse becomes something to build on instead of something to sit under. Without meaning to, I had made myself responsible for producing insight.

If what I wrote felt strong, I felt accomplished.

If it felt simple, I felt behind.

Both reactions assumed the same thing — that the power rested with me.

That's a heavy way to approach Scripture.

One day I caught myself mid-read and asked a different question: What is God already saying here? That question reset the room. The Bible is not a rough draft waiting for my commentary. It is not a launching pad for my creativity. It is God speaking.

When I open Scripture, I am stepping into something alive and active before I ever respond to it. Hebrews tells us the Word of God is living and active. Living things move. Active things accomplish something. That is true whether I write about it or not.

God speaks first.

I respond.

That order matters.

We Are Responders, Not Initiators

When you forget that order, devotional writing becomes exhausting.

You start scanning instead of listening. You begin collecting phrases instead of absorbing truth. The verse slowly turns into content instead of communication.

That drift is subtle — but it is real.

Remembering that we are responders protects us from two extremes. The first is pride. When something you write sounds insightful, you quietly assume you did something impressive. The second is discouragement. When something sounds simple, you assume you failed.

Both responses assume the impact depended on you.

It didn't.

Scripture already carries its own weight. It names what is broken. It announces what is forgiven. It exposes what needs repentance. It delivers comfort that feels almost too personal to explain. Sometimes it does all of that in the same paragraph.

Your role is not to amplify it.

Your role is to notice it.

Devotional writing is simply putting words to what the Word is already doing.

Starting With Life or Starting With the Text

There are two very normal entry points into Scripture.

Sometimes you open your Bible because it is part of your daily rhythm. You are reading through a book of the Bible. The verse is simply there in front of you. You didn't go searching for it. It found you.

Other times, you open Scripture because something in your life feels loud. You are anxious. Grateful. Confused. Waiting. You search for a Psalm. You look up a promise. You flip to a passage someone mentioned in a sermon.

Both doorways are legitimate.

Your life may guide where you turn.

But once the verse is open, it leads.

You do not decide what it says. You do not bend it to match what you were hoping for. You read carefully. You stay in context. You let it correct you if it needs to. You let it comfort you if it offers comfort.

Your circumstances may open the conversation.

The Word determines what is true inside it.

That keeps devotional writing steady. It allows the text to shape you instead of becoming shaped by you.

Grace Before Effort

There is something deeply freeing about remembering that God speaks first.

Before you reflect.

Before you apply.

Before you pray.

He speaks.

Grace precedes effort. That rhythm runs through all of Scripture. God calls. God promises. God acts. We respond.

Devotional writing follows that same pattern.

You are not generating spiritual depth. You are receiving it. You are not manufacturing transformation. You are participating in it.

When that settles in, the pressure eases. You are not performing. You are practicing attention.

You open the Word.

You read it carefully.

You notice what it is doing.

You respond honestly.

That is a much lighter place to write from.

And it is the only place devotional writing actually works.

Pause Here

When you open your Bible, do you feel like you need to come away with something impressive?

What would change if you simply expected to listen?

Try This

Open to a familiar passage and read it slowly twice.

Before writing anything else, answer this in one clear sentence:

What is God saying here?

Keep it simple.

Keep it anchored.

Keep it honest.

Keep it plain.

Chapter 2
What Is a Devotion (And What It Isn't)?

At some point, most of us get weird about the word devotion.

It sounds official. Serious. Possibly intimidating. Like you need soft piano music playing in the background and a perfectly timed story about a sunrise.

That assumption alone is enough to make people close the notebook before they ever start.

So, let's simplify this.

A devotion isn't a sermon. You are not preaching to a congregation. You are not outlining three points and crafting a closing illustration. A sermon carries a different responsibility. A devotion is smaller and more personal. It is you responding to what you heard in Scripture.

A devotion isn't a diary entry either. A diary begins with you. A devotion begins with the Word. Your experience absolutely matters, but it comes second. The verse leads. Your life responds.

It is also not a theology paper. No thesis statement required. No footnotes. No need to prove you have cross-referenced five passages and consulted three commentaries. Depth is wonderful. But depth does not require academic tone.

So, what is it?

It is attention.

It is you reading a verse and asking, "What is God saying here, and how does that land in my actual life?"

That's it.

Anchored, Not Decorative

One of the most common drifts in devotional writing is using Scripture as decoration. A verse appears at the top, but the reflection underneath could have been attached to almost anything.

I've done this.

I once wrote an entire page that felt thoughtful and reflective. When I reread it, I realized something uncomfortable: the verse could have disappeared, and nothing would have changed. I had written around it, not from it.

That was a gentle wake-up call.

The verse is not decoration. It is the foundation.

If Scripture could be removed from your reflection without affecting the meaning, something has drifted. Devotional writing grows out of the text. It does not replace it.

That does not mean every sentence must quote the verse directly. It means the ideas, tone, and direction of your reflection are clearly anchored in what was actually said.

Faithfulness over flair.

The Verse Leads

Whether you start with daily reading or with a specific need, the same principle applies; once the verse is open, it leads.

Sometimes the Word will affirm what you're feeling. Sometimes it will challenge it. Sometimes it will reframe it entirely.

That is not a problem.

That is the point.

Scripture is not there to echo your current mood. It is there to speak truth into it.

Your emotions are real. Your circumstances matter. But they do not define what is true.

The Word does.

When you let the verse lead, devotional writing becomes steadier. It becomes less about producing something inspirational and more about acknowledging what is already there.

You are not inventing insight.

You are recognizing it.

Pause Here

When you picture "a devotion," what comes to mind? Does that picture feel inviting — or intimidating?

Have you ever written something that drifted away from the verse? What would it look like to anchor yourself more intentionally?

Try This

Take one short verse.

Write two sentences about what it actually says — not what it reminds you of, not how it makes you feel, but what it says.

Then write one sentence about how that truth meets your life.

Read it back and circle the words that connect most clearly to the verse itself.

That is your anchor.

Keep it small.

Keep it simple.

Chapter 3

You Don't Have to Sound "Spiritual"

Somewhere along the way, many of us picked up a voice we use only when talking about God.

It's slightly elevated. Slightly polished. Slightly different from how we actually speak to other human beings. The sentences get longer. The tone gets softer. The vocabulary shifts.

You know the voice.

It sounds... devotional.

And while there's nothing wrong with thoughtful language, sometimes that "church voice" creates distance instead of depth. If you would never say, "I find myself wrestling deeply with the complexities of my inward disposition" in real life, you probably don't need to write it in a devotion either.

Yeah. Me neither.

Devotional writing isn't about sounding spiritual. It's about being honest.

There's a difference.

Honest Beats Polished

King David wrote, "You delight in truth in the inward being" (Psalm 51:6). That line matters. God is not impressed by polished phrasing. He delights in truth — inward, real, unfiltered truth.

That should take some pressure off.

Spiritual language can sometimes act like a filter. It smooths things out. It makes them sound tidy. Honest language lets things stay a little raw when they need to be. It allows you to admit confusion. It allows you to say, "I don't understand this yet." It allows you to write, "This verse makes me uncomfortable."

That kind of honesty is far more useful than a paragraph of abstract language.

Paul talks about making an "open statement of the truth" (2 Corinthians 4:2). Not a dressed-up version. Not something tweaked to sound impressive. Just the truth, plainly stated.

That's a beautiful model for devotional writing.

Write Like You Actually Speak

One of the most freeing discoveries in devotional writing is this: your personality does not disappear when you open Scripture.

If you are straightforward, write straightforwardly.

If you are reflective, lean into that.

If you occasionally use humor, that can show up too.

The goal is not to flatten your voice into something generic. The goal is clarity.

And clarity sounds like you.

This does not mean being flippant. It means being real. There is a difference between reverence and stiffness. Reverence honors God. Stiffness usually comes from insecurity.

You do not need to elevate your vocabulary to elevate the truth.

The Word stands on its own.

Avoiding Christian Clichés

We all have phrases we default to.

"God really laid this on my heart."

"I just feel so blessed."

"He showed up in a big way."

Those statements may be sincere. But in writing, they can become vague if we stop there. When you catch yourself using a phrase like that, pause and go one step further.

What does that actually mean?

What did the verse say?

What changed?

What promise did you see?

Instead of "I felt blessed," maybe it becomes, "This verse reminded me that I am not carrying this alone." Instead of "God showed up," maybe it becomes, "This promise steadied me when I was anxious."

Specificity builds clarity.

Clarity builds trust.

Simple Is Not Shallow

There is another subtle trap here. Sometimes we assume that if our reflection sounds simple, it must not be deep.

That's not true.

"I struggle to trust God when I cannot see the outcome" says far more than a paragraph full of abstract spiritual language. Plain honesty often lands harder than poetic phrasing.

You are not being graded on eloquence.

You are practicing attentiveness.

Some days your reflection will feel layered. Other days it will be one clear sentence. Both count. Both can be faithful.

Remember: the power of a devotion does not come from the tone you use. It comes from the Word you are responding to.

You do not have to sound profound.

You have to sound real.

Pause Here

When you write about faith, does your tone change? Do you reach for words you would not normally use?

What would it feel like to write exactly the way you speak?

Try This

Choose a verse and write a short reflection as if you were explaining it to a close friend over coffee.

No fancy phrasing.

No dramatic build-up.

Just clarity.

Chapter 4

Law and Gospel (Without Making It Weird)

The words "Law" and "Gospel" can sound intimidating, especially when we start talking about them in the context of devotional writing. But trust me — understanding these two things is huge for deepening your reflections.

And the best part? It's not complicated.

At the heart of Lutheran theology is a simple truth: the Law shows us what is broken, and the Gospel shows us what is healed.

That's it. Boom. Done.

What the Law Does

The Law is God's Word that tells us what to do. It shows us the commands and the expectations, and it calls us to live according to God's will.

But here's the thing: The Law can't save you.

The Law tells you to love your neighbor, but it doesn't give you the power to do it. It calls you to be holy, but it doesn't make you holy. It shows you how far you've fallen, but it doesn't lift you up.

That's its job.

The Law **exposes**.

It convicts. It shows us what we can't do and what we should've done. The Law never lies. It's clear, unrelenting, and straight to the point.

It's the "you've messed up" part of your reflection.

Here's where it gets uncomfortable: The Law tells you that you cannot save yourself. And it's right.

You will never be enough on your own. I won't either. You'll fall short. I'll fall short. And when you sit with the Law, it brings that sting — that moment when you realize you can't do it all on your own.

But here's the kicker: that's good news in the long run. It prepares you for the next step.

What the Gospel Does

The Gospel, however, is the good news. And here's the part that brings everything together: The Gospel shows us that Jesus has already done everything necessary for our salvation.

The Gospel says, *"You can't do it. But Jesus did."*

The Gospel is not about you.

It's all about Jesus.

It's the grace side of the equation.

Jesus lived the perfect life. Jesus died for you. Jesus rose again. Jesus did it all. All the work. All the saving. All the healing.

Jesus doesn't just tell you to love your neighbor. He loved you first. And that love covers everything.

You don't have to fix yourself. You don't have to be perfect. Jesus is enough.

That is the Gospel.

The Law says, "You're guilty."

The Gospel says, "You're forgiven."

The Law says, "You should do more."

The Gospel says, "It is finished."

Why Devotions Can't End in "Try Harder"

Here's the thing: In devotional writing, we can't just stop with the Law. We can't just sit in the "you've messed up" part and leave it at that. Because that's not the full story.

It's only half the truth. And half-truths can feel like condemnation. We need the whole picture.

Yes, the Law convicts. But the Gospel heals.

It's so tempting to finish a devotion with "Try harder," but that isn't the Gospel.

The Gospel doesn't leave you hanging. It doesn't just say, "Good luck with that." It says, "Here is Jesus. He has done it all. Rest in that."

When we write devotionally, we have to bring both of these together — not in some weird theological tension, but in balance. The Law shows us where we need grace, and the Gospel is the grace we need.

The Gospel says, "Yes, you messed up. But here's what Jesus did about it."

Keeping Christ Central

If your devotion doesn't have Jesus in it, you're missing the whole point.

The Law is always going to show you where you need improvement.

The Gospel is always going to show you where Jesus already made the way.

But Christ is always the hero.

A devotion centered on the Law alone can make you feel like a failure.

A devotion centered on the Gospel alone can feel like cheap grace.

The key is to let both speak — but always with Christ at the center. Always point back to Jesus. He is the reason you can reflect, the reason you have grace, and the reason your writing can actually bring healing.

Pause Here

Can you feel the difference between trying harder and resting in grace?

How does focusing on Jesus change your devotional writing?

Try This

Write a short reflection. Start with a verse that convicts (the Law).

Then, in the next paragraph, write how Jesus fulfills that Law (the Gospel).

Notice how much freer your writing feels when you remember that Jesus already did the work.

Before we jump into structure, take a breath. You have already done something important. You've let go of the pressure to perform. You've remembered that God speaks *first* and you get to *respond*. That changes *everything*. Nothing complicated or over-the-top. Just a clear rhythm you can return to when your brain starts overthinking it. Let's build that next.

PART II: THE STRUCTURE

Chapter 5

Choosing a Verse Without Overthinking It

This is where people freeze.

You open your Bible and immediately think, Okay... but where do I start?

Sixty-six books. Thousands of verses. Poetry. Prophecy. Letters. Law. Narrative. Apocalyptic imagery that feels like a fever dream.

It can feel like too much.

So, let's simplify it.

You do not need the perfect verse.

You need a verse that is in front of you.

Sometimes that means using your daily reading. Sometimes it means revisiting something from Sunday's sermon. Sometimes it means turning to a Psalm because your heart feels fragile that day.

All of that is normal.

But here's the guardrail: wherever you begin, stay there long enough to actually listen.

All Scripture Means All Scripture

Paul writes in 2 Timothy 3:16–17 that "All Scripture is breathed out by God and profitable."

Not just the comforting parts.
Not just the easy parts.
Not just the Instagrammable (is that a word?) parts.

All Scripture.

That means you are not hunting for a motivational quote. You are stepping into something purposeful. Even the verses that convict. Even the ones that confuse you at first. Even the ones that don't immediately feel inspiring.

If it's Scripture, it's useful.

That should take some pressure off.

Read More Than One Sentence

One of the easiest mistakes to make is cherry-picking.

You find a sentence that sounds good on its own and build something around it without noticing what comes before or after. Sometimes that works. Often it drifts.

Context is kindness.

Before reflecting, read at least a few verses before and after. Who is speaking? To whom? Is this a promise? A command? A lament? A warning? A description?

Nehemiah 8:8 describes how the people "read from the book... clearly, and they gave the sense, so that the people understood."

That's what you're doing here.

You're not grabbing slogans.

You're listening for meaning.

Don't Force Depth

There's also a subtle temptation to hunt for something "deep."

Resist that.

Some of the strongest devotions grow out of familiar verses. Psalm 23. John 3:16. Romans 8:1. The familiarity doesn't weaken them. It often strengthens the personal connection.

Depth does not come from obscurity. Depth comes from attention. If a phrase lingers, that's usually enough.

Is there a command that feels uncomfortable?
A promise that feels personal?
A contrast that stands out?

Pay attention to the tug.

Then slow down.

Let the Verse Lead

Here's where Law and Gospel still matter.

Some verses confront you. That's the Law doing its work.

Some verses comfort you. That's the Gospel doing its work.

Some do both.

Do not rush past either.

If the verse exposes something, sit there long enough to admit it. If it comforts you, sit there long enough to receive it.

Do not immediately turn it into a self-improvement project.

Let it speak first.

Always.

Start Small

If you feel overwhelmed, choose a short passage instead of a single fragment. Three to five verses are often better than one isolated sentence.

Write it out by hand if you can. Slowing your body down often slows your thoughts. Psalm 1 describes the blessed person as one who "meditates" on the law of the Lord. Meditation in Scripture isn't mystical fog. It's steady attention.

Read it once.

Read it again.

Ask one simple question:

What is actually being said here?

Not what I've always assumed it meant.

Not what I wish it said.

What does it actually say?

That question alone will keep you grounded.

Pause Here

When choosing a verse, do you rush? Do you scan for something that sounds usable?

What would change if you trusted that whatever passage is in front of you is already purposeful?

Practice: Choosing a Verse

Choose one short passage today; not just a single sentence, but a small section (three to five verses is ideal).

Read a few verses before and after it so you understand what is happening around it. Ask simple grounding questions:

• Who is speaking?
• Who is being addressed?
• Is this a command, a promise, a warning, a lament, a description?
• Is this Law, Gospel, or both?

Notice the setting and the tone. Is Jesus teaching? Is Paul writing to a church? Is this a Psalm prayed in distress? Context matters because meaning lives inside it.

Now answer this in writing:

What stands out and why?

Keep your answer simple. Do not build the devotion yet. Do not apply it yet. Just notice. Absorb. Reflect.

If you feel stuck, try writing the passage out by hand. (I do this almost every single time, no shame.) Slowing your body down often slows your thoughts. Psalm 1 describes the blessed person as one who "meditates" on the law of the Lord. Meditation in Scripture is not mystical fog. It is steady attention.

Start there.

Chapter 6

Writing the Reflection

You've chosen a verse.

Now you're staring at the page.

This is usually the moment where one of two things happens. Either you write half a page in three minutes and hope something in there sounds meaningful, or you sit there thinking, "I have absolutely nothing to say."

I've done both.

Here's what I learned the hard way: the reflection does not start with your opinion.

It starts with observation.

Observation First

Before you decide what the verse means for your life, look at what it actually says.

Slow down enough to absorb it.

Are there repeated words?
Is there a contrast?

A command?

A promise?

A description of who God is?

James writes about the person who "looks intently into the perfect law, the law of liberty" (James 1:25). That phrase "looks intently" matters. This isn't casual scanning. This is focused *attention*.

You are not mining the verse for content.

You are letting it speak.

Take something familiar like, "The Lord is my shepherd; I shall not want" (Psalm 23:1). Slow it down. It doesn't say the Lord acts like a shepherd. It says He *is* one. It also says *my* shepherd. That one word makes it personal.

Observation feels basic.

It's not.

Observation protects you from drifting into general spiritual commentary that could attach to almost any verse. It keeps the reflection anchored.

Faithfulness begins with *noticing*.

Then Personal Connection

Only after you observe clearly do you move into connection.

Where does this meet me?

Does it confront something?

Comfort something?
Expose something?
Correct something?

If the verse commands something you haven't done, that is the Law doing its work. Here's where Law and Gospel show up again. Romans 3:20 reminds us that *through the law comes knowledge of sin.*

Sit with that for a moment.

Don't stay there alone, though.

If the verse proclaims what *Christ* has done, that is the Gospel doing its work. Let it comfort you. Let it steady you. Let it speak louder than your performance. Romans 8:1 declares, *"There is therefore now no condemnation for those who are in Christ Jesus."*

> *That changes the tone of everything.*

A faithful reflection allows both to speak when both are present.

Conviction without Christ becomes crushing.
Grace without truth becomes vague.

The Word holds them together.

So should your reflection.

Avoiding Drift

Here's how drift happens.

You start with a verse about trusting God. Within three paragraphs, you are writing about time management, productivity, and how to wake up earlier.

Sometimes that connection works. Often, it wanders.

A simple question will guard you:

> *Can someone clearly see how this reflection grows out of this verse?*

If the Scripture could disappear and your reflection would still stand untouched, something has drifted.

That is not condemnation.

It's *calibration*.

Go back to the text. Read it again. Let it tighten your focus.

Christ at the Center

Here is the most important guardrail.

Where is Jesus in this?

Not every verse mentions Him explicitly. But all of Scripture ultimately points to Him. Luke 24:27 reminds us how Scripture they testified about Him.

> *And beginning with Moses and all the Prophets, he interpreted to them in all the Scriptures the things concerning himself.*

If the verse *convicts* you, ask how Christ fulfilled what you failed to fulfill.

If the verse *comforts* you, ask how that comfort flows from Christ's finished work.

If the verse *commands* something, remember that Jesus obeyed perfectly where you do not.

He's not an afterthought.

He's the center.

A reflection that ends with "I need to try harder" is incomplete. A reflection that ends with *"Christ has done this for me, and now I respond"* is anchored and deeply freeing.

Keep It Clear

You don't need five paragraphs or a dramatic story.
You don't need to explain everything the verse could possibly mean.

You need one clear thread.

Clarity is important to your reader and to yourself.

If you feel stuck, try this sentence starter:

> *"This verse shows me..."*

Finish it plainly.

Then ask:

> *"Where does that truth meet my life right now?"*

That often becomes the backbone of your reflection.

Short and anchored is stronger than long and wandering.

Pause Here

When you write reflections, do you move quickly to application before fully observing the text?

What would change if you lingered in the verse a little longer?

Practice: Writing the Reflection

Choose your passage.

Write two or three simple observations about what it actually says. Stay concrete.

Identify whether you see Law, Gospel, or both.

Write one short paragraph describing where this truth meets your life right now.

End by asking: Where is Christ in this?

Read it back and underline the sentence most clearly tied to the verse.

That sentence is your anchor.

Build from there.

Chapter 7

Asking Questions That Actually Help

I'll admit something right up front: writing reflection questions does not come naturally to me. I think in statements. I like clarity. I like landing the point and letting it stand. Turning that into a question used to feel like I was assigning homework at the end of something meaningful.

If you feel that way too, you're not alone.

When done well, questions aren't homework. They are *invitations*. They slow you down just enough to let the truth settle instead of skim across the surface.

In Luke 2:19, after everything surrounding Jesus' birth, we're told that Mary *"treasured up all these things, pondering them in her heart."* That word pondering matters.

> She wasn't explaining everything.
> She wasn't producing insight.
> She was turning it over quietly.

That is the posture we're aiming for. Reflection questions, at their best, help you ponder rather than perform.

The easiest way to write a good question is not to begin with a question at all. Start with a clear sentence from your reflection.

Suppose you wrote, *"God is patient with me even when I resist Him."* That sentence already carries weight. From there, you can gently turn it into a question:

> *Where have I seen God's patience with me lately?*
> *What makes me resist Him?*
> *What would trusting Him sooner look like?*

Notice what happened. You didn't invent something complicated. You simply opened space for the truth you already wrote to settle more deeply.

Not every devotion needs questions. When they're helpful, they tend to fall into three natural patterns. Some questions help you stay anchored in the text itself:

What stands out?
What is repeated?
Is this Law, Gospel, or both?
What does this reveal about God?

These kinds of questions guard against drift and keep your reflection tied to the actual words of Scripture.

Other questions bring the truth closer to home.

Where does this meet my life?
Where do I struggle with this?
Where have I already seen this at work?

The tone here matters. These are invitations to awareness, not accusations. There is a difference between conviction and condemnation. The Law exposes what is broken, but Romans 8:1 reminds us *there is no condemnation for those who are in Christ*

Jesus. A healthy question allows the Law to do its work while still leading you toward grace.

The most important questions, however, are the ones that move you *toward* Christ.

What does this show me about Jesus?
How does Christ fulfill what this verse commands?
Where do I see grace here?

If your reflection questions never turn in His direction, they will slowly become exercises in self-analysis.

> *Self-analysis alone does not save. Jesus does.*

It's easy to slip into guilt-driven questions without realizing it.

> *Why am I so bad at this?*
> *Why don't I trust God more?*
> *Why can't I get this right?*

Those questions might sound reflective, but they can quickly become heavy. Instead, try asking,

> *"What does this struggle reveal about my need for Christ?"*

That shift keeps Law and Gospel together. Conviction remains, but hope stands beside it.

Devotional questions are not a checklist. They are not five steps to improvement or a spiritual diagnostic quiz. They are simply space; space to notice, to confess, to receive. Sometimes one clear question is enough.

More questions do not equal more depth. Clarity does.

If questions genuinely feel forced for you, you're allowed to skip them. Some devotions end beautifully *without* them. The goal is not to complete a template. The goal is *attentiveness*.

One honest question that opens space for Christ is more than enough.

Practice: Crafting Questions

Look at your reflection from the previous chapter.

Choose one sentence that clearly connects to the verse.

Rewrite that sentence as one simple question.

Read it out loud. Does it invite thought without feeling heavy?

If it does, you are on the right track.

Chapter 8

Writing an Honest Prayer

Let me say this loud and clear for the people in the back:

I'm not naturally good at praying.

The words are usually in my head somewhere. I know what I mean. I know how I feel. I just don't always organize it well. If you ask me to pray on the spot, I will probably sound slightly awkward. Ok, very awkward. Possibly repetitive. Definitely not poetic. It's guaranteed to get weird the longer I talk.

I tell my confirmation students that all the time because the pressure to sound impressive in prayer is *real... but it's unnecessary*

God isn't grading vocabulary. He's not evaluating sentence structure. He's not impressed by eloquence.

He is your Father.
He wants you to talk to Him.

Period.

Prayer Is Not a Performance

Jesus actually addresses this directly. In Matthew 6:7, He says,

> *"When you pray, do not heap up empty phrases as the Gentiles do, for they think that they will be heard for their many words."*

Many words do not equal better prayer.
Fancy words do not equal deeper faith.
Performance does not equal sincerity.

If anything, performance can create *distance*. It can make prayer feel like something you do *for God* instead of something you do *with Him*.

Prayer is not a speech.

It is conversation.

Conversation assumes relationship.

The Spirit Is Already Helping

If that sounds familiar, you are in good company.

Romans 8:26 says,

> *"... the Spirit helps us in our weakness. For we do not know what to pray for as we ought, but the Spirit himself intercedes for us with groanings too deep for words."*

That includes awkward prayers.

That includes rambling prayers.

That includes "I don't even know what to say right now" prayers.

The Spirit is *already helping* before you form the sentence.

That should take enormous pressure off.

If you feel weak in prayer, you're in the exact place Scripture assumes you'll be.

Let the Verse Shape the Prayer

Prayer in a devotion isn't about being naturally fluent. It's not a random add-on at the end. It grows naturally out of the verse you just reflected on. The prayer section is simply you turning your reflection into conversation with God.

If the verse exposed something in you, tell Him.

If it comforted you, thank Him.

If it challenged you, ask for help.

If you're still confused, admit that.

Borrow the language of the text whenever possible. If the verse says God is faithful, pray, *"Father, thank You for being faithful when I am not."* If it calls you not to fear, pray, *"Help me trust You here."*

You do not need to clean it up first.

Scripture gives you the vocabulary.

The Psalms are full of this. Raw honesty. Joy. Lament. Confession. Praise. David does not sanitize his prayers. He pours them out. Psalm 62:8 says,

> *"Pour out your heart before him; God is a refuge for us."*

Pouring out does *not* sound polished, does it?

It sounds *real*.

You're not inventing something new.
You're *responding*.

The Lord's Prayer Is Enough

When the disciples asked Jesus how to pray, He didn't give them a performance model. He gave them words.

> *"Our Father in heaven…"*

The Lord's Prayer (Matthew 6:9–13) is not just something we memorize. It's a pattern. It reminds us who God is, what matters most, and where our daily needs fit.

Notice how grounded it is:

> Your name.
> Your kingdom.
> Your will.

Then:

> Give us.
> Forgive us.
> Lead us.
> Deliver us.

It's simple.

It's direct.

It's enough.

If you ever feel stuck writing a prayer in a devotion, you can echo that pattern. Begin with *who God is*. Acknowledge what He has done. Ask for what you need. Trust Him with what you cannot control.

That is faithful prayer.

Keep It Short. Keep It Honest.

A devotional prayer does not need to be long.

Two sentences can be enough.

Sometimes one sentence is enough.

> *"Father, I struggle to trust You here. Help me."*

That counts.

> *"Lord, thank You for forgiving me again."*

That counts.

> *"In Jesus' name, Amen."*

That counts too.

The goal is not length. It is sincerity.

You are responding to what God has already spoken. You are not trying to move Him emotionally. You are resting in what He has promised.

Prayer in a devotion is simply turning reflection into conversation.

Nothing fancy.

Nothing theatrical.

Just you and your Father.

Pause Here

When you pray, do you feel pressure to sound spiritual?

What would change if you believed God already knows what you're trying to say?

Practice: Writing an Honest Prayer

That simple pattern can steady your words when your brain feels messy.

Remember, God already knows what you're trying to say. Writing the prayer isn't for Him to understand you better. It's for you to slow down enough to *mean* what you're saying.

It doesn't need to be polished.

It needs to be *real*.

I may have mentioned that before.

If it does, it's enough.

Chapter 9

Crafting the One-Liner

I'm going to be honest again.

Concise is *not* my default setting.

Those who know me, stop laughing.

Give me space and I will happily write a full paragraph. Ask me to say it in one sentence and suddenly I feel pressure. However, I do like this part. I like playing with words. I like turning a truth over and seeing if I can say it cleanly.

The one-liner is not a slogan. It is not a dramatic mic-drop moment. It is simply the clearest thread running through your reflection. Well, ok, it *could* be a mic-drop.

After you write your reflection and prayer, ask yourself: What was the *main truth* here? *If someone remembered only one sentence, what would you want it to be?*

That sentence is your one-liner.

Psalm 119:130 says, "*The unfolding of your words gives light.*" Light is not complicated. It's clear. It reveals what's already there. A good one-liner does that. It shines light on the heart of the verse without adding clutter.

It should stay close to the verse. It should sound like you. It should be clear without being cheesy.

For example, if your reflection focused on God's patience, your one-liner might be:

God stays patient with me, even when I push back.

That's not flashy.
It's just focused.

This is the place where you can enjoy wordplay if that feels natural. You don't need to force being clever. Some one-liners are straightforward. Others carry a little rhythm. Both are fine. Roll with it.

The only thing to avoid is stretching for something that sounds inspirational but disconnects from the verse. If it could be printed on a random coffee mug and still make sense *without* Scripture, it may be drifting away from its intention.

A helpful test is this: Read your one-liner and then read the verse again. Do they clearly belong together? If the connection feels strong, you're good.

Keep it simple.

Keep it grounded.

Sometimes the one-liner comes easily, sometimes it takes days to appear. Other times you may need to rewrite it two or three times. That's totally normal.

Play with it. Trim extra words. Rearrange the order. Read it out loud.

You're not trying to impress anyone.

You're trying to capture the *heart* of what you just learned.

And yes, you're allowed to have a little fun with this.

Practice: One-Liners

Look at your reflection and prayer.

Write one sentence that captures the central truth of your verse. Keep it clear. Keep it connected to the text.

If it feels clunky at first, revise it once or twice. Read it out loud. Does it sound like you?

If it does, keep it.

PART III: WRITING WITH DEPTH

Chapter 10

Fully Worked Sample Devotions

Sample Devotion 1: Comfort

Verse

"The Lord is near to the brokenhearted and saves the crushed in spirit." Psalm 34:18

Reflection

There are days when you are functioning... but not fine.

There are days when you are showing up... but running on empty.

There are days when you hold everything together... and quietly fall apart inside.

There are days when you answer "I'm good, thanks" ... and it's anything but true.

However, you show up. You answer messages. You keep commitments. You smile in the grocery store. On the outside, everything looks status quo. On the inside, something feels heavy and quiet and tired.

This verse doesn't say the Lord is near to the *impressive*. It doesn't say He is near to the *composed*. It says He's near to the *brokenhearted*.

That changes the room, does it not?

Brokenhearted isn't fancy language. It's *honest* language. It covers grief, disappointment, betrayal, private fears. It describes the quiet ache of prayers that feel unanswered.

The promise here isn't that you'll avoid those things. The promise is *God's presence*.

> *"The Lord is near."*

Not observing from a distance. Not waiting for you to recover. *Near.*

Sometimes we think we need to fix ourselves before drawing close to God. This verse reverses that instinct. The very place you feel weakest is the place He draws closest.

The second half of the verse says He saves the crushed in spirit. That word crushed carries weight (pun intended). It suggests pressure. Exhaustion. The feeling of being pressed down by circumstances you did *not* choose.

He doesn't shame that condition.
That doesn't always remove the circumstance.
He meets you in it.

If your heart feels heavy today, this verse doesn't demand strength from you. It reminds you of His *nearness*.

That's enough for today.

Let's work with this…

Author Note:

Notice how the reflection stayed close to the actual words of the verse: "brokenhearted," "near," "crushed." Each paragraph grew out of language already right there in the text. That keeps the devotion grounded rather than drifting into general encouragement.

Optional Reflection Question

Where in my life do I feel pressure or heaviness right now, and how might God's nearness change how I carry it?

Author Note:

This question does not shame. It invites awareness. It flows directly from the reflection and keeps the Gospel promise central.

Prayer

Father, You see what feels heavy in me. Thank You for drawing near instead of pulling away. Help me remember Your presence when my heart feels tired. Anchor me in Your nearness today. Amen.

Author Note:

The prayer borrows the language of the verse: near, heavy, anchor. It responds directly to the reflection rather than introducing a new topic.

One-Liner

God comes closest to me where I feel weakest.

Author Note:

The one-liner captures the main truth without sounding inspirational for its own sake. It echoes the verse clearly.

Sample Devotion 2: Identity

Verse

"I have called you by name, you are mine." Isaiah 43:1

Reflection

I can make my identity weird in about five minutes if I am not careful. All it takes is one comparison, one unfinished task, one comment that lingers in my brain longer than it should. Suddenly I am measuring myself by my productivity (or lack thereof), usefulness (ditto), or whether anyone noticed what I did (most often I'm praying they did not). It doesn't take much for my sense of worth to start teetering.

This verse is refreshingly steadying. It almost feels like a big hug.

"I have called you by name, you are mine."

That's not vague language. It's specific and personal. God doesn't call you by your performance, your role, or your current mood. He calls you by name. That means *known, seen, intentionally claimed*.

Then comes the anchor: "You are mine."

Not "you might be mine *if...*" Not "you are mine on your best days." Just mine.

Some days I operate as if I'm freelancing in the universe, responsible for building and maintaining my own value. Yes, I hear how ridiculous that sounds. This verse corrects that gently but firmly. Belonging is not something you manufacture. It's something declared over you.

Whether it's a productive day or a messy one.

Whether you feel confident or completely behind.

You are still *His*.

That doesn't change just because your performance does. It doesn't shift with public opinion. It doesn't shrink when you feel small.

Identity grounded in *belonging* is steadier than identity built on performance.

Author Note:

See how I kept coming back to the exact words in the verse? "Called by name." "You are mine." I didn't wander into a full lecture on identity. I just stayed close to the text. Then I didn't have to work so hard to sound deep.

Optional Reflection Question

Where have I been tying my worth to performance instead of resting in belonging?

Author Note:

The question didn't come out of nowhere. It grew right out of the tension in the first paragraph. It invites honesty without turning into a guilt trip. That's the goal. We want reflection, not shame.

Prayer

Father, I slip so easily into measuring myself by what I accomplish. Thank You for calling me by name and claiming me as Yours. Help me live today like I actually believe that's enough. Amen.

Author Note:

The prayer doesn't introduce anything new. It simply turns the reflection into conversation with God. Short. Clear. Connected to the verse. That's all it needs to be.

One-Liner

I don't have to prove what God's already declared.

Author Note:

The one-liner isn't trying to be clever. It just says the main truth plainly. If it sounds like something you would actually say out loud, you're on the right track.

Sample Devotion 3: Repentance

Verse

"Create in me a clean heart, O God, and renew a right spirit within me." Psalm 51:10

Reflection

Can I admit something?

Sometimes the problem isn't the situation. It's my attitude inside it. Not always. Not every time, but sometimes. Ok, *often*.

There are moments when I replay a conversation and realize I wasn't as patient as I thought. Or I catch myself justifying a grudge because it feels easier than letting it go. Or I notice how quickly I get defensive instead of listening.

Psalm 51 isn't polished. David isn't asking God to make things smoother. He's asking for a clean heart.

"Create in me a clean heart."

Not tweak it. Not manage it better. *Create*.

That word gently admits something: *I can't fix this on my own.*

If I could, I wouldn't need to ask.

That's where grace slips in. Even repentance is grounded in mercy. David isn't trying to earn his way back. He's asking God to do what only God can do.

"Renew a right spirit within me."

Not a perfect one. Not a flawless one. *A right one.* A spirit turned back toward God instead of inward on itself.

Repentance doesn't mean entering a downward shame spiral. It means being honest about what's sitting in your heart and bringing it to light. It means saying, "This part of me needs help."

There is something freeing about that.

You don't have to defend everything. You don't have to explain it. You don't have to minimize it.

You can just ask and let God create.

Author Note:

Notice how the reflection doesn't start with David. It starts with something personal and honest. That makes space for the reader before we even get to the verse. Then the reflection keeps circling back to specific words in the text: create, clean heart, renew, right spirit.

When you're writing about repentance, resist the urge to lecture. Let Scripture carry the weight.

Optional Reflection Question

Is there anything in my heart right now that I've been excusing instead of confessing?

Author Note:

The question grows naturally out of the examples in the first few paragraphs: impatience, grudges, defensiveness. It's specific without being harsh. It invites honesty, not humiliation.

Prayer

Father, You already see what's in me; where I've been impatient, proud, defensive, or just tired and snappy. Create in me what I can't create myself. Renew what has drifted. Thank You for Your mercy and grace. Amen.

Author Note:

The prayer doesn't try to sound impressive. It simply echoes the verse: create, renew. When you feel stuck writing a prayer, lift words straight from the Scripture you just reflected on.

One-Liner

I need to stop managing and start asking.

Author Note:

The one-liner doesn't summarize repentance as a concept. Good one-liners usually reflect the turning point of the devotion. They don't need to define doctrine. They just need to say the main truth plainly.

Sample Devotion 4 — Calling

Verse

"For we are His workmanship, created in Christ Jesus for good works, which God prepared beforehand, that we should walk in them." Ephesians 2:10

Reflection

The phrase "find your calling" can make perfectly normal people feel like they missed a memo.

It sounds like there is a hidden envelope somewhere with your name on it and you just have not located it yet. So, you start looking harder. Praying harder. Comparing harder.

Meanwhile, your actual life is happening right in front of you.

Paul says we are His workmanship. That means you are not an afterthought. God did not throw your personality together and hope it works out. He made you on purpose.

Then he says we were created for good works that God prepared beforehand.

Beforehand.

That part always makes me pause. It means I am not inventing my purpose from scratch every morning. I am stepping into something *already prepared*, and that takes some pressure off.

Calling does not always look like a big reveal. Sometimes it looks like answering the phone when you would rather not. Sometimes it looks like choosing patience when you're two seconds away from being snappy. Sometimes it looks like being consistent in something small and unglamorous.

We tend to think if it doesn't feel dramatic, it must not count; but Paul uses the word *walk*.

Walk isn't dramatic. Walk is daily. Walk is one faithful step at a time.

Maybe calling is less about discovering a hidden destiny and more about noticing where God already has you planted.

You are His workmanship *first*.

The good works are not how you earn that title. *They flow from it.*

You don't have to chase purpose down; just take the next faithful step.

Optional Reflection Question

Where might God already have me placed that I keep overlooking?

Prayer

Father, I can make calling bigger and more complicated than it needs to be. Thank You for preparing good works ahead of me instead of asking *me* to invent them. Help me notice what You've already placed in front of me and to walk in it faithfully. Amen.

One-Liner

Maybe calling is less about finding something new and more about walking where God already has me.

Sample Devotion 5 — Hope

Verse

"Because of the Lord's great love we are not consumed, for His mercies never fail. They are new every morning; great is Your faithfulness." Lamentations 3:22–23

Reflection

It helps to remember where these words were written.

Lamentations is not a cheerful book. It's grief on paper. Loss. Disappointment. Things not turning out the way anyone hoped they would. Right there, in the middle of it, comes this line:

Because of the Lord's great love we are not consumed.

Not "everything is fine."

Not "this doesn't hurt."

Not "give it time and it'll be perfect."

Not consumed.

Consumed is what happens when worry is on a loop, when regret sits too long, and when uncertainty starts narrating your story.

Jeremiah doesn't deny the pain around him. He doesn't pretend the situation is bright. He anchors himself in something else: *the Lord's love.*

Then he adds: *His mercies never fail. They are new every morning.*

New every morning means you don't have to hoard strength for tomorrow. You don't have to drag yesterday's leftovers into today. Today has its own supply.

Hope, in this verse, is not loud optimism.

It says,

> *"This may be heavy, but it will not consume me."*

> *"God's faithfulness doesn't fluctuate with my circumstances."*

It's constant and reliable.

Hope doesn't negate reality. It steadies you within it.

If today feels unfinished or uncertain, this verse doesn't rush you through it. It reminds you that you are not walking through it *alone*, and you are *never* walking without mercy.

Optional Reflection Question

What feels like it might "consume" me right now, and what would it look like to trust God's mercy?

Prayer

Father, some days feel heavier than I expected. Thank You that Your mercy meets me fresh each morning. Help me trust that I am not

consumed and that Your faithfulness is steadier than what I see.
Amen.

One-Liner

I am not consumed. God's mercy meets me again tomorrow.

Chapter 11

Common Devotional Writing Mistakes

Let's just say this up front: if you recognize yourself in any of the following pages, congratulations, you're normal.

Every devotional writer has a phase.

There's the "accidental sermon outline" phase.

The "everything is a life lesson" phase.

The "I will now solve your entire spiritual life in three bullet points" phase.

If you've written any of those, welcome to the club. I have the membership card.

The goal of this chapter is not to shame you. It's to sharpen you.

Here's the truth: when we handle God's Word publicly, even in a short devotion — we are doing something weighty. Not dramatic. Not elite. But weighty. We're putting words around the Word.

And that deserves care.

The good news? Most devotional writing mistakes aren't theological disasters. They're just subtle drifts. Tiny shifts that slowly turn Christ-centered reflection into self-improvement advice, emotional hype, or something that sounds spiritual but doesn't actually say much.

So, we're going to lovingly call a few of those out.

Not to embarrass you, but to help you write better.

More importantly, to help you keep Jesus at the center instead of accidentally replacing Him with "Do better."

Let's start with one of the most common reflexes of all.

Turning Everything into "Try Harder"

This one sneaks in so easily.

You read a verse about trusting God, and by the end of your reflection it somehow turns into a self-improvement plan.

Trust more.

Worry less.

Pray harder.

Do better.

Now listen, none of those things are bad. The Bible absolutely calls us to trust and obey. That's real. That matters.

If your devotion ends there, though, something subtle has happened.

The spotlight shifts.

Instead of resting in what *Jesus* has done, the focus lands on what *we need to do* next. What *we need to fix*. What *we need to improve*.

Suddenly what started as comfort feels like a spiritual progress report.

There's a very common Christian writing reflex that goes like this:

- Read a verse.
- Find the action word.
- Turn it into a command.
- Add three helpful tips.
- Wrap it up with, "You've got this!"

And just like that, Scripture becomes a pep talk.

It sounds encouraging. It sounds practical. It can even sound spiritual.

However, it can slowly drift away from the heart of the Gospel.

Here's the simple truth:

> *Christianity does not start with your effort.*
> *It starts with God's grace.*

Ephesians 2:8–9 says we are *saved by grace through faith, not by works*. That means your relationship with God is *not* built on how well you perform. *It's built on what Christ has already done.*

Yes, good works matter. The very next verse says we were created for them. Good works are fruit.

Fruit grows *because* the tree is alive.

Fruit doesn't *make* the tree alive.

If we aren't careful, we can take every verse and turn it into something the reader needs to achieve. Not every verse is a command, though. Many verses are simply telling us something beautiful and steady and true about God.

Take Psalm 23: *"The Lord is my shepherd; I shall not want."*

It's very tempting to write:

"Since God is your shepherd, you need to trust Him more. Stop worrying. Stay close."

Those thoughts aren't *wrong* but notice how quickly the comfort turns into homework.

Instead of letting the reader breathe in the promise that the Lord Himself leads, provides, protects, we rush to give them something to do.

That's where devotion writing can start to feel burdensome.

There is a place for challenge. There is a place for correction. But promise comes first.

Sometimes the most faithful thing you can do as a devotional writer is simply let God's promise stand.

Let it comfort.

Let it speak.

Let it be enough.

If your reflections regularly leave the reader feeling more pressure than peace, pause for a second.

Ask: Is this verse mainly telling me what to do — or is it telling me what God has done?

If God is speaking promise, you don't need to improve it.

You just need to pass it on.

And in a Christian devotion, the final note should never be "try harder."

It should be Christ.

Always.

Turning Every Story into "Be More Like Them"

You read a story in Scripture, and almost without thinking, your brain goes straight to:

"What's the lesson for my life?"

David and Goliath becomes:

"Face your giants."

Daniel in the lion's den becomes:

"Stand strong under pressure."

Esther becomes:

"Be brave when it's hard."

Listen, those ideas aren't terrible. Courage is good. Faithfulness is good. Bravery is good, but that's not the whole story.

When every Bible story turns into *"Here's how you can be better,"* we accidentally make the Bible mostly about *us*, and it's not.

The Bible is not mainly a collection of role models. It's a story of *rescue*.

David isn't just a brave shepherd boy showing you how to conquer your personal problems. He's a picture. A shadow. A preview.

> *He defeats an enemy that God's people couldn't defeat on their own.*

That should sound familiar.

Daniel surviving the lions isn't just about you surviving awkward meetings or stressful seasons. *It's about God preserving His people when destruction looks certain.*

Esther isn't simply teaching you confidence. It's about God working through unlikely people to protect His covenant promises.

The thread running through Scripture is not "try harder and be braver."

It's this:

> *God saves.*

> *Again and again and again.*

Every one of those stories ultimately points forward to the greater King, the One who defeats the enemy we could never defeat.

That King is Jesus.

If every devotion ends with "Be more like David," we've shrunk the Bible down to a character-development seminar.

If we let the story breathe, we start to see something bigger.

David points to Christ.

Daniel points to Christ.

Esther points to Christ.

The story is about rescue.

Your rescue.

My rescue.

Our rescue.

...with Jesus at the center of it.

Always.

Forgetting the Cross

Sometimes devotions get serious fast. We talk about pride. We talk about fear. We talk about selfishness, compromise, impatience, envy... all the things. Sure, that can be good. Honest is good. Naming sin is good. Scripture does that all the time.

If we stop there, it gets heavy.

The Law tells the truth. It shows us what's broken. Romans 3:23 says all have sinned. That includes me. That includes you. No one gets a gold star here, and that part matters.

So does the cross.

Romans 5:8 says that while we were still sinners, Christ died for us. Not after we cleaned ourselves up. Not after we promised to do better. Not after we had a really good week. While we were still sinners.

If we write a devotion that names sin but never mentions the Savior, we've only told half the story. If we point out the *failure* but never speak *forgiveness*, we've left the reader standing in the problem without showing them the *rescue*.

That's not biblical honesty. That's unfinished work.

The cross is not an *optional add-on* to a devotion. It's not the "nice ending." It's the center. Yes, we should speak truth. Yes, we should be clear about what's broken. Every time we expose sin, *we must also point to the One who paid for it.*

Otherwise, people walk away thinking mostly about themselves: *my* pride, *my* fear, *my* weakness, *my* failure; instead of thinking about *Christ and His mercy, His obedience, His sacrifice, His finished work.*

A Christian devotion should never leave someone staring only at their sin.
It should move them to the cross.

That's where the weight lifts and where hope lives..

Making Grace Too Small

There's another drift that feels softer but matters just as much.

Sometimes we skip over sin entirely and go straight to encouragement.

"You're doing great."

"Just keep believing."

"You've got this."

Now, encouragement is not wrong. We all need it. Hebrews 10:24 tells us *"to stir up one another to love and good works"*. Life is heavy. Faith can feel exhausting. Kind words are a *gift*.

Grace is more than encouragement.
Grace is not just God saying, "Keep your chin up."
Grace is God stepping in to do what we could not do ourselves.

The Bible says in Ephesians 2:1 that we were *"dead in the trespasses and sins."* Dead. Not discouraged. Not slightly off track. Dead. A few verses later it says, *"But God, being rich in mercy... made us alive together with Christ"* (Ephesians 2:4–5).

That's grace.

Jesus didn't come simply to make you feel better about yourself. He came to save you. Matthew 1:21 says, *"He will save His people from their sins."* That's the mission. That's the rescue.

If we write devotions that only say, "You're fine. Just keep going," without ever acknowledging what needed saving, grace starts to shrink. It becomes soft background comfort instead of life-changing rescue.

The cross wasn't necessary because we were *slightly stressed*.

It was necessary because we were *lost*.

Romans 5:8 reminds us that "*while we were still sinners, Christ died for us*".

> *That means grace is not casual.*
> *It is costly.*
> *It required the Son of God to suffer, bleed, and die.*
> *When we understand that, grace doesn't feel small.*
> *It feels astonishing.*

A devotion can absolutely be hopeful. It can be gentle. It can be full of comfort. It should not turn grace into a motivational slogan or a pat on the back.

Grace is not God cheering from the sidelines.

It is God entering the battle, carrying the weight, and declaring, "It is finished."

That's not small.

That's *everything*.

Saying Things That Sound Biblical but Aren't

We've all heard phrases that sound incredibly spiritual.

They get posted on mugs.

They show up on Instagram.

They're said with great confidence.

The only problem?

They're not actually in the Bible.

→ *"God helps those who help themselves."*

That one sounds wise. Responsible. Mature. Guess what? It's not Scripture. In fact, the Gospel says the *opposite*. Romans 5:6 says, *"While we were still weak, at the right time Christ died for the ungodly."*

God helps the helpless. That's the whole point.

→ *"God will never give you more than you can handle."*

People usually mean this kindly. They're trying to comfort someone. But Paul writes in 2 Corinthians 1:8 that he was "so utterly burdened beyond our strength that we despaired of life itself." That sounds like more than he could handle.

And then he explains why: "That was to make us rely not on ourselves but on God who raises the dead" (2 Corinthians 1:9).

The point wasn't Paul's strength. It was God's.

→ *"Follow your heart."*

That one feels empowering. But Jeremiah 17:9 says *"The heart is deceitful above all things, and desperately sick"*. Left on its own, it doesn't always lead us toward truth. Scripture points us instead to follow Christ, to trust His Word, to walk by the Spirit.

Here's the issue: phrases like these often mean well. No one is trying to twist Scripture on purpose. In devotional writing, however, we are handling something *precious*. We don't want to lean on what *sounds spiritual*.

We want to lean on what God has actually said.

The Word is strong enough.

Hebrews 4:12 says the Word of God is living and active. It doesn't need our upgrades. It doesn't need catchy slogans to make it powerful.

Sometimes the most faithful thing you can write is simply what the Bible *actually says*.

Not the polished version.

Not the popular version.

Not the Pinterest version.

Just the Word.

It's already strong.

It doesn't need our help.

When Devotion Turns into Self-Help

There's a version of Christian writing that still uses Bible verses but slowly becomes life coaching. It sounds positive. It feels practical.

It looks helpful. Underneath it, though, the message quietly shifts into, "Here's how to improve yourself."

Read more. Try harder. Fix your habits. Be more disciplined. Wake up earlier. Pray longer. Do better this time.

None of those are bad goals. Growth matters. Discipline matters. Scripture calls us to maturity. Yet here's the subtle drift: *self-help begins with you, while the Gospel begins with Christ.*

Self-help says, "You can do this if you try." The Gospel says, "You cannot save yourself and you don't have to." That difference changes everything.

Galatians 3:3 asks, "*Having begun by the Spirit, are you now being perfected by the flesh?*" In other words, if your faith started with God's grace, why would you think it continues by your effort?

Colossians 2:6 echoes that same idea: "*As you received Christ Jesus the Lord, so walk in Him.*" We received Him by grace, through faith, not by performance.

> *The Christian life doesn't start with grace and then switch into self-improvement mode.*
>
> *It stays grace from beginning to end.*

When devotion slowly becomes Christian-flavored motivation, it might inspire someone for a week. It might energize them on Monday morning, but it won't carry them through grief. It won't steady them in shame. It won't hold them at 2 a.m. when fear won't let them sleep.

> *Motivation fades. Grace sustains.*

Self-help tells you to climb higher. The Gospel tells you Christ came down.

Self-help hands you a plan. The Gospel points you to a finished work.

Romans 8:1 says there is now *no condemnation for those who are in Christ Jesus*.

Matthew 11:28 records Jesus saying, *"Come to Me... and I will give you rest."* That's not a strategy. That's a Savior.

If your devotion could still stand even if you removed the name of Jesus, pause for a moment. That might be self-help.

A Christian devotion should *collapse* without Him.

He's not an add-on.

He's the whole point.

When We Try to Sound Deep

Sometimes the drift isn't theological at all. It's tonal.

We assume devotion needs to sound profound, so we stretch sentences, stack adjectives, and reach for words we don't normally use. We take a simple truth and wrap it in layers until it feels impressive and slightly exhausting.

We start writing things like, "In the existential tension of our sanctification journey..." when what we really mean is, "Growing in faith can be hard."

Clarity quietly disappears.

Jesus didn't teach that way. He talked about seeds and soil. Sheep and shepherds. Bread and light. Lost coins. Open doors. Things people could see and touch and understand. His teaching had depth, but it also had *clarity*. You didn't need a dictionary to follow Him.

Simple doesn't mean shallow.

Short doesn't mean weak.

Plain doesn't mean unspiritual.

In fact, truth becomes powerful when it is understandable.

Paul says in 1 Corinthians 14:9 that if speech is unclear, "*how will anyone know what is said?*" His concern wasn't sounding impressive. It was being understood. Even in 1 Corinthians 2:1–2, he reminds the church that he didn't come with lofty speech or wisdom, but simply proclaiming *Christ crucified*.

That's the goal.

If someone has to reread your paragraph three times to figure out what you meant, that's not depth. That's fog. Fog doesn't feed anyone.

There's nothing wrong with thoughtful language. There's nothing wrong with careful phrasing. Devotion writing isn't about showcasing your vocabulary. *It's about serving the reader.*

You are not trying to impress.

You are trying to proclaim.

There's a big difference.

When your writing is clear, *Christ shines through it.* When your writing is complicated for the sake of sounding spiritual, the spotlight shifts to you.

This book has been saying from the beginning: He's the point.

Keep the Order Clear

Here is the simplest way to check your writing:

What comes first? Your effort or Christ's work?

That order matters more than you think.

It must always be Christ first.

Titus 3:5 says, *"He saved us, not because of works done by us in righteousness, but according to His own mercy."* That's the foundation.

Salvation is not a reward for effort.

It's an act of mercy and it begins with Him.

Saved first.

Good works follow.

Ephesians 2 says we are saved by grace through faith and then created for good works. The works come *after* the rescue, not before it. *They grow out of what Christ has already done.*

We obey because we are loved.

We serve because we are secure.

We produce fruit because the root is already alive.

When that order flips (even a little bit) everything starts to feel heavy.

      X   Faith becomes pressure.
      X   Obedience becomes proof.
      X   Devotion becomes performance.

Instead, when the order stays clear, something steadies.

      ✓   *Christ has acted.*
      ✓   *Christ has finished the work.*
      ✓   *Christ holds you secure.*

From *that* you live, serve, grow, and write.

If you keep that order clear in your devotions, you will protect both your reader and yourself from a thousand tiny drifts.

Christ first.

Everything else flows from there.

A Gentle Check

When someone finishes reading your devotion, what do they carry with them?

A longer list of things to fix?

Or a clearer picture of Jesus?

That simple question can reveal a lot.

If a reader walks away thinking mostly about what they need to improve, what they failed at, what they should try harder to do, pause and look again. Not with panic. Not with shame. Just with honesty.

If they walk away remembering what Christ has done for them (His mercy, His obedience, His finished work) you're on solid ground.

That's the goal.

Not perfect writing.

Not impressive phrasing.

Not spiritual performance.

Clear proclamation of Jesus.

Every time.

Here's the bottom line in all of this: *you won't do it perfectly*. None of us do. If your instinct is to keep bringing the reader back to Christ (back to the cross, back to the promise) you are headed in the right direction.

That's the check.

It's a gentle one.

Why This Matters

This isn't just about writing technique. It's about what people walk away believing.

Devotional writing shapes hearts. It shapes how people see God. It shapes how they see themselves. When someone reads what you've written, they aren't just evaluating your phrasing. They're absorbing what you're saying about sin, grace, obedience, and Christ.

If someone struggling with guilt reads your devotion and only hears, *"Do better,"* they leave discouraged. They may try harder for a while, but eventually, they'll feel tired.

If someone struggling with pride reads your devotion and only hears *comfort without correction*, they leave unchanged. They may feel affirmed.

They won't feel the need for a Savior.

However, if they hear both truth and grace, something steadies.

If they hear the Law expose what is broken and the Gospel announce what Christ has done about what is broken, they leave grounded.

Not crushed.
Not flattered.
Grounded.

They leave remembering that Jesus is enough.

Enough for their sin.
Enough for their weakness.
Enough for their future.

That's what we want.

Not perfect devotions.

Not clever phrasing.
Not spiritual performance.

Clear proclamation of Christ.

Christ first.
Christ crucified.
Christ risen.

Every time.

Chapter 12

When You Feel Like A Fraud

Let's say this out loud.

At some point, you are going to feel like a fraud.

You'll sit down to write about trust while quietly worrying. You'll write about patience on a day when you've already snapped at someone. You'll reflect on forgiveness while still holding onto something you should probably release. And the thought will creep in:

Who am I to write this?

That question sounds humble. Sometimes, it is.

Sometimes it hides a misunderstanding.

You are not writing as the expert who has conquered sin. You are writing as someone rescued by Christ. There is a difference.

Paul wrote letters about faith, endurance, holiness, and love — and yet he openly called himself the chief of sinners (1 Timothy 1:15). He didn't wait until he was flawless to speak about grace. He spoke as someone who needed it.

You don't write because *you* are perfect.

You write because *Christ is*.

If devotional writing required moral perfection, there would be no devotional writers.

The real question isn't, *"Have I mastered this?"*

It's, *"Is this true?"*

If what you are writing is rooted in Scripture and centered on Christ, then you are not pretending. You are proclaiming.

There's a world of difference between those two things.

There have been days when I've written about patience with tears in my eyes because I knew I hadn't lived it well that morning. It can feel hypocritical. It can feel dishonest. It can feel like you're presenting a version of yourself that hasn't quite caught up yet.

Here's the deeper truth: you are not writing because you've mastered the verse.

You are writing because you need it.

That difference matters.

The Lie of "Qualified Enough"

Somewhere along the way, many of us picked up the idea that we need to be spiritually impressive before we can speak about spiritual things. That we need to be consistently strong before we can talk about faith. That we need to have it all together before we write a single sentence.

We quietly assume there's a level we have to reach.

Once I'm more disciplined.

Once I struggle less.

Once I finally get this right.

Then I'll be qualified.

That's not how the Gospel works.

The Gospel is not for the spiritually impressive.

It's for sinners.

Romans 5:8 says that while we were still sinners, Christ died for us. Not once we cleaned ourselves up. Not once we proved we understood everything. Not once we demonstrated steady growth.

While we were still sinners.

Look, if the Bible were only written by people who had everything figured out, it would be a very short book.

David wrote psalms in the middle of failure. Some of his most honest words came from seasons of guilt, fear, and repentance.

Peter preached Christ after denying Him.

Paul called himself the *chief of sinners* (1 Timothy 1:15) even as he was planting churches and writing Scripture.

They did not write from perfection.

They wrote from mercy.

They wrote as people who had been confronted by their sin and overwhelmed by grace.

Being "qualified" in the Kingdom of God doesn't mean being flawless. It means being *rescued*. Colossians 1:12 says the Father has qualified you to share in the inheritance of the saints. He did the qualifying!

Your role is not to impress anyone with your spiritual résumé.

Your role is to testify to what Christ has done.

You can do that even while you are still being shaped.

Writing as a Beggar

There's a line often connected to Martin Luther that says,

> *"We are beggars; this is true."*

At first that sounds kind of harsh, but it's actually comforting.

A beggar doesn't pretend to have it all together. A beggar doesn't act like they earned the food. A beggar simply receives it.

That's us.

When you write a devotion, you're not the expert standing at the front of the room with all the answers. You're someone who has been given something good, and you're pointing to where it came from.

You're not the source.

You're just someone who received the bread.

That changes the pressure, doesn't it?

When you write about trust while you're still learning to trust, you're not being fake. You're being honest. When you write about patience on a day you didn't handle everything perfectly, you're not pretending to be better than you are.

You're saying, *"This is what God's Word says. And I need it just as much as you do."*

That's not hypocrisy.

That's *humility*.

You're not writing because you've mastered the lesson.

You're writing because you're *hungry* for it.

Beggars are allowed to talk about bread.

Hypocrisy vs. Struggle

There's a big difference between hypocrisy and struggle, and it's important not to mix the two up.

Hypocrisy is pretending you don't struggle. It's acting like you've arrived. It's writing about patience as if you've never raised your voice or talking about trust like you never worry. That's fake, and deep down, everyone can feel it.

Struggle is different. Struggle says, "Yeah... I'm still working on this." It admits the weakness instead of hiding it. It doesn't pretend to be further along than it really is. And then it points to Christ anyway.

If you write about patience and say, "I fail at this more than I'd like, but I'm grateful God doesn't give up on me," that's not hypocrisy. That's honest. That's faith. That's someone who knows they need grace.

Devotional writing isn't a highlight reel of your spiritual wins. It's not you standing on a stage showing off how steady and strong you are. It's you saying, "Here's what God's Word says, and I need it just as much as you do."

You don't have to act like you've mastered the lesson. You just have to tell the truth about it.

Jesus didn't come for people who had it all together. He came for people who knew they didn't. He meets the tired, the frustrated, the ones who feel behind. He meets people in the *middle* of the struggle, not after they've cleaned it up.

Struggle doesn't disqualify you from writing.

Pretending does.

So, if you're still growing, still learning, still tripping over the same things sometimes — welcome. You're in good company.

That's not fraud.

That's faith.

The Accuser's Voice

When you start to feel like a fraud, it's worth slowing down and asking one simple question:

Where is that voice coming from?

Revelation 12:10 calls Satan "the accuser." That's literally what he does.

He accuses. He whispers. He pokes at your weak spots.

Accusation usually sounds like this:

"You're not good enough."

"You don't actually live this out."

"You have no business writing about this."

It's harsh. It's shaming. It doesn't offer a way forward.

Here's something important, though: conviction from the Holy Spirit sounds different.

Conviction says, "Yes, that's sin." Then it leads you somewhere. It leads you to repentance. After repentance, it leads you to Christ.

Accusation leaves you stuck.

Conviction moves you.

Accusation says, "Hide."

Conviction says, "Come to Jesus."

If the thought in your head pushes you toward shame, isolation, or silence, that's not from God. God does not shame His children into hiding.

If the Spirit brings something to your attention and then reminds you of the cross, *that's grace at work.*

Romans 8:1 says, *"There is therefore now no condemnation for those who are in Christ Jesus."*

No condemnation.

Not for imperfect writers.

Not for believers who are still growing.

Not for *you*.

If you belong to Christ, the verdict has already been spoken.

You are forgiven. You are covered. You are His.

So, when that accusing voice tries to tell you that you shouldn't write because you're not good enough, remember this:

The cross has already answered that accusation.

It didn't answer with shame.

It answered with mercy.

Dry Seasons

There will be seasons when you don't feel much.

The verses don't hit the same. Prayer feels weird. You read something that used to move you, and now it just... sits there.

You might even wonder if something's wrong.

It's not.

Faith isn't built on constant emotional highs. It's built on *truth*, and truth doesn't disappear just because your feelings shift.

The Psalms are full of dry seasons. *"Why, O Lord, do You stand far away?"* (Psalm 10:1). That's not a polished, Sunday-morning sentence. That's someone who feels the distance.

Yet the same book keeps coming back to trust.

Dry seasons don't mean you've lost your faith.

They mean you're human.

Sometimes God seems quiet, but quiet doesn't mean absent.

Sometimes the Word feels ordinary, but ordinary doesn't mean powerless.

You may not always feel deeply stirred when you open your Bible. That doesn't mean it isn't working. Isaiah 55:11 reminds us that God's Word does not return empty. It does what He sends it to do whether you feel it in the moment or not.

There will be days when you write and think, "This feels flat." Write anyway.

The strength of a devotion doesn't come from how inspired you felt while typing it.

It comes from the truth it points to.

Your feelings rise and fall.

God's Word doesn't.

Writing When You Don't Feel It

There are going to be days when you just don't feel it.

> You don't feel close to God.

> You don't feel inspired.

> You don't feel "spiritual enough" to be writing anything.

You'll think, "Maybe I should wait until I'm in a better place." Or "I'll write when I feel more connected." Or my personal favorite,

> "I'll start tomorrow."

If you wait until you always feel ready, you're going to wait a long time.

A lot of the time, it's just you, tired, with your Bible open, trying to focus while your brain wanders.

Sometimes writing looks like typing one honest paragraph and thinking, "Well... that's all I've got today."

That's okay.

You don't write because you feel spiritually impressive.

You write because *God's Word is still true*, even on your off days.

> It's true when you're cranky.

> It's true when you're distracted.

> It's true when your faith feels about the size of a mustard seed.

2 Corinthians says we *walk by faith, not by sight*. I'd add: not by mood either.

There's something quietly faithful about showing up anyway. Not to prove you're deep. Not to perform. Just to say, "Lord, I need this again. So, I'm opening Your Word again."

Here's the wild part: sometimes the devotion you almost skipped writing is the one someone else needed most.

You don't need to feel on fire to be faithful.

You just need truth.

Truth doesn't depend on how you feel that day.

Grace Covers the Writer

It's funny how easy it is to write about grace for other people.

You can say, "*God forgives.*"

You can say, "*His mercy is new every morning.*"

You can remind someone else that they're loved.

When it comes to you? That's harder, right?

Somehow, we think we're the exception. Seriously? Have we learned nothing?

Like grace is for the readers... but pressure is for the writer.

That's not how it works.

The same Gospel you point other people to *applies to you, too*.

The forgiveness you describe? *That's yours.*

The mercy you highlight in your devotion? *It covers you.*

The patience of God you write about? *That patience is toward you.*

You don't stand *outside* the promises like a tour guide explaining them. You stand *inside* them.

Saved by grace.
Growing by grace.
Still learning by grace.
Even writing by grace.

When you mess up, *grace covers you.*

When you doubt, *grace covers you.*

When you feel like you shouldn't even be the one typing the words, *grace still covers you.*

You are not writing about something you're *trying to earn.*

You are writing about something you've *already been given.*

That changes the pressure completely.

Why You Keep Writing Anyway

So, what do you do when you feel like a fraud?

You don't quit.

You don't close the Bible and decide you'll come back when you're "better." You don't wait until you feel more consistent, more disciplined, or more impressive.

You remember what this was about in the first place.

Devotional writing isn't about *proving* you've arrived. It's not about showing everyone how spiritually mature you are.

It's about responding to the Word.

That's it.

You open the verse. You let it speak.

If it convicts you, you admit it.

If it comforts you, you receive it.

If it exposes something, you bring it to Christ.

Then you write from that place. Not from a pedestal, but from a seat at the table.

You are not writing because you're spiritually ahead of everyone else.

You're writing because you need Jesus, too.

You need the same grace.

The same mercy.

The same reminder of what He has done. When you write from that place, you're not pretending.

You're participating.

You're joining the long line of imperfect believers who have said,

"Here is what God's Word says. And I'm clinging to it."

That's not fraud.

That's faith.

That's reason enough to keep going.

Chapter 13

Writing About Real Life Without Making It About You

There's nothing wrong with writing about your real life. In fact, you should. If your devotions *never* touch real stress, real mistakes, real family tension, real doubt, or real joy, they can start to feel distant like they were written in a bubble.

God's Word meets us in real life. That's one of my favorite lines (if you haven't figured that out yet!). So yes, write about what actually happened this week. Write about the moment you failed. Write about the hard conversation. Write about the time you saw grace in action.

Here's the important part: *your life is not the point.*

Jesus is.

Your story can be *helpful,* but it is not the hero. If we're not careful, the spotlight can slowly move without us even noticing.

Personal ≠ Self-Centered

Writing personally is not the same thing as writing self-centered.

Personal writing says, "Here's where I struggled, and here's how this verse met me."

Self-centered writing says, "Let me tell you more about me."

There's a difference.

Personal writing connects the reader to truth. Self-centered writing can start to feel like someone else's diary.

> *Here's a simple test: after someone reads your devotion, will they remember Christ more clearly or will they mostly remember your story?*

If your story helps people understand Scripture better, keep it.

If your story becomes the main event, trim it back.

You are not writing to impress people with your vulnerability. You are writing *to point people to Christ*.

Using Story as Illustration, Not Spotlight

Think of your story as a flashlight. It helps people see something. No one stares *at* the light of a flashlight. They look at *what it's shining on*.

> *Your story should shine light on the Word, not replace it.*

You might begin with something like, "This week I realized how impatient I can be." That's honest. That's real. Don't stay there too long, though.

> *Move to the verse.*

Move to what God says.
Move to what Christ has done.

Your life can open the door.

Scripture should walk through it.

When to Share (and When Not To)

Not every detail needs to be shared.

Just because something happened doesn't mean it belongs in a devotion. Some stories are still too raw. Some involve other people who didn't choose to be part of your writing. Some moments are better processed privately before they're published.

Ask yourself: Is this helpful? Is this wise? Is this loving?

You don't have to bleed on the page to be authentic.

You can be honest without oversharing.

There is strength in knowing when to hold something back.

Writing from Anger, Grief, or Confusion

There will be times when you're writing in the middle of something hard.

You're angry.
You're hurt.
You're confused.
That's real life.

The Bible is full of people crying out in pain. The Psalms aren't neat and tidy. They're honest. Even in the middle of their confusion, they turn toward God.

If you're writing from a place of pain, make sure you're still pointing to *Him*.

> *It's okay to say, "I don't understand."*

> *It's okay to admit you're struggling.*

Let Scripture speak *louder* than your emotions. Let Christ remain steady, even when *you don't feel* steady.

Letting Christ Be the Hero

At the end of the day, you are not the hero of your devotion.

Even when you share something vulnerable.

Even when you admit failure.

Even when you tell a powerful story.

> *The hero is always Christ.*

He is the One who forgives.

He is the One who strengthens.

He is the One who saves.

Your role is smaller and that's actually rather freeing.

You don't have to wrap everything up perfectly. You don't have to sound impressive. You don't have to make yourself look wise.

You just have to point.

     Point to the Word.

     Point to the cross.

     Point to Jesus.

Then step out of the spotlight.

Chapter 14

Finding Your Devotional Rhythm

One of the fastest ways to burn out is to try to write like someone else.

You see someone posting a devotion every single morning at 5:00 a.m., and suddenly you think that's the standard. You decide you're going to do the same. For three days, you do great.

On day four, you're tired.

On day six, you're annoyed.

By day ten, you're done.

That's not failure.

That's trying to live in *someone else's rhythm*.

God did not assign you someone else's pace.

Some people write daily. Some write weekly. Some write in seasons. Some write in bursts when inspiration hits. There isn't one holy schedule.

The goal is not to impress anyone with some sort of consistency.

The goal is to *stay connected to the Word*.

Daily vs. Weekly Writing

If writing daily helps you stay in Scripture, great. If it starts to feel rushed or forced, slow down.

Weekly writing might give you more space to think and pray. It might allow the verse to settle deeper before you put words on the page.

> There is no spiritual medal for frequency.

> Faithfulness matters more than volume.

Ask yourself: *What pace allows me to stay thoughtful and grounded instead of frantic?*

That's probably your rhythm.

Writing in Busy Seasons

There will be seasons when life is loud.

> Work is heavy.
> Family needs more from you.
> Your calendar is full.
> You might not have long stretches of quiet time.

That doesn't mean you have to stop completely. It might mean your devotions get shorter. Simpler. More direct.

Sometimes one honest paragraph is enough.

You don't need five pages. You don't need polished transitions. You need *truth*.

Let your writing adjust to your season instead of quitting altogether.

Writing in Quiet Seasons

Then there will be slower seasons.

> More margin.

> More time.

> More space to think.

Those seasons can be beautiful for writing. You may find yourself going deeper. Exploring more context. Sitting longer with a passage.

Enjoy those seasons.

Don't assume they'll last forever and don't build expectations you can't maintain when life speeds up again.

Every season has its own rhythm.

Building a Sustainable Practice

If you want to keep writing long-term, build something you can *actually sustain*.

Maybe that means setting one realistic writing day each week.

Maybe it means keeping a small notebook where you jot down thoughts during the week and shape them later.

Maybe it means writing in shorter formats during busy months and longer reflections when you have room.

The key is this: don't build a system that only works when life is perfect.

Life is rarely perfect.

Give yourself room to be human.

When to Take a Break

There may also be times when you need to step back for a while.

Not because you failed.

Not because you're unqualified.

But because *your soul needs rest*.

Even Jesus withdrew to quiet places to pray. Rest is not weakness. It's wisdom.

If writing starts to feel forced, dry, or resentful, *pause*.

Sit under the Word without trying to produce something from it. Let yourself receive without immediately turning it into content.

You are a believer *first*.

A writer *second*.

The health of your soul matters more than your output.

At the end of the day, devotional writing isn't about proving how steady you are.

It's about staying close to Christ over time.

Find a rhythm that keeps you near Him.

Not rushed.

Not pressured.

Not burned out.

Just steady.

Steady is more powerful than you think.

PART IV: PRACTICE & APPLICATION

Chapter 15

Extended Practice Templates

By now, you've seen the structure.

You've watched it happen five times.

You've practiced pieces of it.

Now it's your turn.

These pages aren't here to test you. They're here to give you room. Use them slowly. Skip around if you want. Repeat the same verse twice if that helps you dig deeper. There's no devotional police.

Each template follows the same rhythm as the samples. Keep it simple. Keep it honest. You don't have to fill every line. You just have to begin. These pages are where it shifts from "That makes sense" to "Okay, I'm doing it."

If you feel stuck, start small. Write one sentence. Then another. You don't need momentum to begin. You just need a verse and a pen.

Some of these may turn into devotions you keep. Some may feel rough. Both are normal.

This is practice. Practice is allowed to be imperfect.

Devotion Practice Template 1

Verse

(Write out the verse/the portion you're focusing on.)

____

____

Reflection

(What do you notice in the verse? What words stand out? Where
does this meet your life right now?)

____

____

____

____

____

____

____

Optional Reflection Question

____

____

Prayer

____

____

One-Liner

____

Devotion Practice Template 2

Verse

(Write out the verse/the portion you're focusing on.)

____

____

Reflection

(What do you notice in the verse? What words stand out? Where
does this meet your life right now?)

____

____

____

____

____

____

____

____

Optional Reflection Question

____

____

Prayer

____

____

One-Liner

____

Devotion Practice Template 3

Verse

(Write out the verse/the portion you're focusing on.)

____

____

Reflection

(What do you notice in the verse? What words stand out? Where does this meet your life right now?)

____

____

____

____

____

____

____

Optional Reflection Question

____

____

Prayer

____

____

One-Liner

____

Devotion Practice Template 4

Verse

(Write out the verse/the portion you're focusing on.)

____

____

Reflection

(What do you notice in the verse? What words stand out? Where does this meet your life right now?)

____

____

____

____

____

____

____

Optional Reflection Question

____

____

Prayer

____

____

One-Liner

____

Devotion Practice Template 5

Verse

(Write out the verse/the portion you're focusing on.)

____

____

Reflection

(What do you notice in the verse? What words stand out? Where does this meet your life right now?)

____

____

____

____

____

____

____

Optional Reflection Question

____

____

Prayer

____

____

One-Liner

____

Devotion Practice Template 6

Verse

(Write out the verse/the portion you're focusing on.)

____

____

Reflection

(What do you notice in the verse? What words stand out? Where does this meet your life right now?)

____

____

____

____

____

____

____

Optional Reflection Question

____

____

Prayer

____

____

One-Liner

____

Devotion Practice Template 7

Verse

(Write out the verse/the portion you're focusing on.)

____

____

Reflection

(What do you notice in the verse? What words stand out? Where does this meet your life right now?)

____

____

____

____

____

____

____

Optional Reflection Question

____

____

Prayer

____

____

One-Liner

____

Devotion Practice Template 8

Verse

(Write out the verse/the portion you're focusing on.)

____

____

Reflection

(What do you notice in the verse? What words stand out? Where does this meet your life right now?)

____

____

____

____

____

____

____

Optional Reflection Question

____

____

Prayer

____

____

One-Liner

____

Devotion Practice Template 9

Verse

(Write out the verse/the portion you're focusing on.)

____

____

Reflection

(What do you notice in the verse? What words stand out? Where does this meet your life right now?)

____

____

____

____

____

____

____

Optional Reflection Question

____

____

Prayer

____

____

One-Liner

____

Devotion Practice Template 10

Verse

(Write out the verse/the portion you're focusing on.)

____

____

Reflection

(What do you notice in the verse? What words stand out? Where does this meet your life right now?)

____

____

____

____

____

____

____

____

Optional Reflection Question

____

____

Prayer

____

____

One-Liner

____

Chapter 16

30-Day From Verse to Voice Challenge

You do not need thirty days of motivation.

You need one day and a pen.

This challenge is not about producing thirty polished devotions. It is about building the *habit of responding* to Scripture consistently.

Some days you will write a full page.

Some days you will write three sentences.

Some days you will stare at the verse for a while and that will just have to do.

The goal is *not volume*.

The goal is *response*.

Thirty days is long enough to build confidence and short enough to feel doable.

Keep it simple:

> Read.
> Notice.
> Respond.
> Pray.
> Capture one sentence.

That's it.

How the Challenge Works

Each day:

• Choose one verse (use the prompt list or your own).

• Write a short reflection (even 5–6 sentences count).

• Add an optional question if it flows naturally.

• Write a brief prayer.

• Finish with a one-liner.

If you miss a day, do not restart the calendar. Just continue.

This is learning and growth, not perfection.

The 30-Day Challenge

This isn't about perfection; it's about showing up. Each day is a small step in listening and responding to God's Word.

Day	Verse	Reflection	Prayer	One-liner
1	_______________	☐	☐	☐
2	_______________	☐	☐	☐
3	_______________	☐	☐	☐
4	_______________	☐	☐	☐
5	_______________	☐	☐	☐
6	_______________	☐	☐	☐
7	_______________	☐	☐	☐
8	_______________	☐	☐	☐
9	_______________	☐	☐	☐
10	_______________	☐	☐	☐
11	_______________	☐	☐	☐
12	_______________	☐	☐	☐
13	_______________	☐	☐	☐
14	_______________	☐	☐	☐
15	_______________	☐	☐	☐

Day	Verse	Reflection	Prayer	One-liner
16	______________	☐	☐	☐
17	______________	☐	☐	☐
18	______________	☐	☐	☐
19	______________	☐	☐	☐
20	______________	☐	☐	☐
21	______________	☐	☐	☐
22	______________	☐	☐	☐
23	______________	☐	☐	☐
24	______________	☐	☐	☐
25	______________	☐	☐	☐
26	______________	☐	☐	☐
27	______________	☐	☐	☐
28	______________	☐	☐	☐
29	______________	☐	☐	☐
30	______________	☐	☐	☐

Whether you completed all 30 days or just a handful, you showed up. That matters. Keep listening. Keep responding. The Word does the work, and the habit of listening is taking root.

Verse Prompt List

Of course you are welcome to use any verses, but here's a 30-day set balanced across grace, identity, comfort, wisdom, calling, hope:

Day 1 – Psalm 46:10

Day 2 – Lamentations 3:22–23

Day 3 – Romans 8:1

Day 4 – Proverbs 3:5–6

Day 5 – Psalm 34:18

Day 6 – Ephesians 2:8–9

Day 7 – Isaiah 43:1

Day 8 – Philippians 1:6

Day 9 – John 15:5

Day 10 – James 1:5

Day 11 – Psalm 51:10

Day 12 – Romans 8:28

Day 13 – Psalm 16:11

Day 14 – 1 Peter 5:7

Day 15 – Joshua 1:9

Day 16 – 2 Corinthians 12:9

Day 17 – Isaiah 41:10

Day 18 – Matthew 11:28

Day 19 – Romans 12:1–2

Day 20 – Psalm 139:13–14

Day 21 – Zephaniah 3:17

Day 22 – 1 John 3:1

Day 23 – Colossians 3:23

Day 24 – Hebrews 4:16

Day 25 – Psalm 23:1

Day 26 – Galatians 5:22–23

Day 27 – Deuteronomy 31:6

Day 28 – John 14:27

Day 29 – Philippians 4:6–7

Day 30 – Romans 15:13

Keep Going Encouragement

If you reach Day 12 and feel like quitting, that's normal.

Habits resist forming at first. Your brain will tell you this is unnecessary. Your schedule will suddenly feel very full.

Keep going anyway.

You aren't trying to impress God. You are building the muscle of *listening*.

Some of your entries will feel strong. Some will feel flat. That does not mean the Word stopped working.

Faithfulness is rarely dramatic.

Thirty small responses to Scripture can quietly reshape how you hear God's voice in everyday life.

When you finish Day 30, *do not evaluate your writing*. Look at your consistency.

You showed up.

That matters.

Chapter 17

If You Want to Use This in a Small Group

You don't need a leadership certificate or a teaching degree to use this book with a group.

You don't need a binder.

You don't need a slideshow.

You don't need a color-coded schedule.

You need a Bible, this book, and a willingness to listen.

That's it.

If you can ask a question and let silence sit for a moment without panicking, you can lead this.

Let's keep this simple.

(Snacks optional. Highly encouraged)

What a Basic Group Night Could Look Like

Here's one very uncomplicated rhythm:

1. Open in prayer. Keep it short.
2. Read the chosen verse out loud.

3.   Give everyone 10–15 minutes to write quietly.

4.   Invite volunteers to share part of their reflection.

5.   Close in prayer.

That's a full meeting.

You do not need to fix anyone's writing.
You do not need to evaluate theological depth.
You do not need to have better answers than everyone else.

Your role is not to impress.

Your role is to create space.

Space where the Word is read.
Space where people think.
Space where people respond.

The Holy Spirit does not need you to be dazzling.

He works through the Word.

What Not to Overcomplicate

You do not need:

• A deep dive into Greek verbs (cool as that sounds)

• A ten-minute mini-sermon before writing

• Perfect participation from everyone

• A dramatic emotional response

If the verse is read and people respond honestly, the Word is doing its work.

Resist the temptation to over-teach. When leaders get nervous, they talk more. When leaders talk more, participants write less.

> This is not a performance space.

> It's a practice space.

Let people wrestle with the text.

Let them think. Let them be quiet.

You don't have to fill every gap

Protecting Law and Gospel Clarity

This matters.

When people start sharing, conversations can drift quickly into:

"So, what we all need to do is *try harder*."

That's your cue.

Gently bring it back.

If someone shares guilt, remind them of grace.
If someone shares pride, don't erase truth.
If someone feels crushed, point them to Christ.

The goal is not to leave people with a longer to-do list.

The goal is to leave people remembering what Jesus has done.

You don't need to use theological terms. Just ask simple questions:

> Where do you see promise in this verse?
> What has Christ done here?
> What is God saying before He asks us to do anything?

Keep that order clear.

Christ first.

Always.

If the Group Gets Quiet

Silence is *not* failure.

Sometimes people are thinking. Sometimes they are processing. Sometimes they are just tired.

Give the room a moment.

If you need a gentle nudge, ask:

> *"What word stood out to you?"*

> *"Did anything in the verse feel comforting or challenging?"*

> *"What sentence did you underline?"*

Simple questions. Open space.

Then let it breathe.

You do not have to rescue every quiet moment.

If Someone Shares Something Heavy

This will happen eventually.

Someone may admit doubt. Or guilt. Or something painful. Hear this now:

> *You are not their therapist.*

You are not required to solve their life in five minutes.

You *can* say:

> *"Thank you for sharing that."*

> *"I'm glad you said that out loud."*

> *"Let's remember what this verse says."*

Then bring it back to Christ.

Grace.

Promise.

Hope.

That's your lane.

If You're Leading Teens

Keep the writing shorter.

Lower the pressure.

Model honesty first.

Teens will respond to authenticity faster than to polish. If you share a small, real example of your own writing process, including where you struggled, it gives them permission to *try*.

You do not need to simplify theology.

You just need to simplify expectations.

If You're Leading Adults

Remind them this is not a comparison exercise.

Some will write a page.

Some will write three lines.

Both count.

The goal is not literary excellence.

It's *attentiveness*.

Sometimes adults need permission to *not be* impressive.

A Gentle Structure for Multi-Week Groups

If you're meeting weekly, try this:

Week 1 – Read Chapter 1–3, practice one template
Week 2 – Focus on Reflection writing
Week 3 – Focus on Prayer
Week 4 – Focus on One-liners
Week 5 – Share full devotions
Week 6 – Begin the 30-Day Challenge together

Or simplify even more:

Choose one verse each week and just write.

You literally cannot do this wrong.

Final Encouragement for Leaders

You are not responsible for transformation.

You are responsible for creating space where Scripture is read and responded to.

That's enough.

> *You don't have to produce spiritual breakthroughs.*
>
> *You don't have to manage everyone's growth.*
>
> *You open the Word.*
>
> *You make space.*
>
> *You point to Christ.*

Let the Word do the work.

It always does.

Final Thoughts

The Word Will Keep Working

If there is one thing I hope you carry from this book, it's this:

The pressure was never on you.

Not to sound profound.

Not to write something impressive.

Not to uncover hidden meaning in every verse.

The Word of God does not depend on *your brilliance*. It does not need your perfect grammar or exquisite vocabulary. It does not wait for you to sharpen your phrasing before it begins to move.

God speaks first.

We respond.

That rhythm has not changed. It will not change.

It does not rest on your shoulders.

If you have written one devotion in this book, you have practiced listening. If you have written thirty, you have practiced consistency. If you have stumbled through awkward sentences and half-formed prayers, you have still done something *meaningful*.

You paid attention.

That alone matters more than you think.

There will be days when your writing feels clear and days when it feels thin. Days when you feel steady and days when you feel distracted. Neither one determines whether God is working.

Scripture has never required polish to accomplish its purpose.

It convicts.

It comforts.

It corrects.

It anchors.

It renews.

Often quietly. Often slowly.

Most of God's work in us is not dramatic.

It's steady.

Your role is *not* to manufacture transformation.

Your role is to stay near the Word.

Open it.

Read it.

Notice it.

Respond *honestly*.

Then trust that what God begins in you, He will continue. Not because you are disciplined enough, but because He is *faithful*.

The Word will keep working long after you close this book.

It will work on tired days.

It will work in joyful seasons.

It will work when you feel strong.

It will work when you feel small.

It does not retire when you finish a chapter.

It keeps speaking.

You keep responding.

That's the life of faith.

> Not flashy.
> Not perfect.
> Steady.

So, keep *listening*.

Keep *opening* your Bible.

Keep *writing* when you can.

Keep *receiving* grace when you fail.

Keep *pointing* to Christ.

One faithful step at a time.

If you ever feel unsure again about your writing, about your voice, about your growth, remember this:

The Word does the work.

It always has.

It always will.

You are safely held inside that promise.

God bless you as you continue

walking

writing,

and responding.

He is not finished with you.

Not even close.

A Personal Note

Before you close this book, I want to say something to you directly.

Not as a teacher. Not as a so-called "writer." Just me, Kim, as a fellow believer who also opens her Bible and sometimes stares at the page longer than she'd like to admit.

I did not write this because I have it all figured out. I wrote it because I need the same rhythm I invited you into.

God speaks.

I respond.

Some days that response is clear and confident.

Some days it's messy and short.

Some days it's a half-finished prayer scribbled in the margin.

He keeps speaking... and I'm for it.

That has changed my life more than any writing technique ever could.

If this book helped you slow down, helped you feel less pressure, helped you see that you don't have to sound impressive to be faithful, then I'm grateful.

Not because of the words on these pages, but because you leaned in.

You paid attention.
You practiced listening.

That matters.

>*More than metrics.*

>*More than page counts.*

>*More than polished sentences.*

It matters that you showed up.

If you forget everything else in this book, remember this:

>*You are not trying to become*
>*a better devotional writer*
>*so that God will draw near to you.*

He already has.

You are responding to a God who speaks *first*.

That changes everything.

Thank you for reading.

Thank you for writing.

Thank you for walking this rhythm with me.

God bless you!

Commissioning the Reader

Now go.

Not to perform. Not to impress. Not to prove that you learned something.

Go to *listen*.

Open your Bible tomorrow like you did inside these pages. Read slowly. Notice what stands out. Let the Law tell the truth and

let the Gospel have the final word.

Write when you can. Rest when you need to. Lead if God gives you the space. Encourage someone else to try.

When you feel unsure (and you will) remember what anchored this entire book:

God speaks first.

You respond.

That's enough.

You don't need a platform.

You don't need a perfect voice.

You don't need flawless consistency.

You need the Word.

... and you already know where to find it.

So, keep opening it. Keep receiving it. Keep pointing to Christ.

Not dramatically, not perfectly, but steadily.

One faithful response at a time.

Trust that the Word will keep working.

It always has.

It always will.

Now go write.

Appendix

Bible Verses By Category

GRACE

John 3:16 – For God so loved the world, that he gave his only Son, that whoever believes in him should not perish but have eternal life.

Romans 5:8 – but God shows his love for us in that while we were still sinners, Christ died for us.

Romans 8:1 – There is therefore now no condemnation for those who are in Christ Jesus.

Ephesians 2:8–9 – For by grace you have been saved through faith. And this is not your own doing; it is the gift of God, not a result of works, so that no one may boast.

2 Corinthians 5:17 – Therefore, if anyone is in Christ, he is a new creation. The old has passed away; behold, the new has come.

Ephesians 1:7 – In him we have redemption through his blood, the forgiveness of our trespasses, according to the riches of his grace

1 John 1:7 – But if we walk in the light, as he is in the light, we have fellowship with one another, and the blood of Jesus his Son cleanses us from all sin.

1 John 5:11 – And this is the testimony, that God gave us eternal life, and this life is in his Son

COMFORT

Psalm 34:18 – The Lord is near to the brokenhearted and saves the crushed in spirit.

Lamentations 3:22–23 – The steadfast love of the Lord never ceases; his mercies never come to an end; they are new every morning; great is your faithfulness.

Matthew 11:28 – Come to me, all who labor and are heavy laden, and I will give you rest.

John 14:27 – Peace I leave with you; my peace I give to you. Not as the world gives do I give to you. Let not your hearts be troubled, neither let them be afraid

1 Peter 5:7 – casting all your anxieties on him, because he cares for you.

Revelation 21:4 – He will wipe away every tear from their eyes, and death shall be no more, neither shall there be mourning, nor crying, nor pain anymore, for the former things have passed away.

2 Corinthians 1:3–4 – Blessed be the God and Father of our Lord Jesus Christ, the Father of mercies and God of all comfort, who comforts us in all our affliction, so that we may be able to comfort those who are in any affliction, with the comfort with which we ourselves are comforted by God.

Psalm 55:22 – Cast your burden on the Lord, and he will sustain you; he will never permit the righteous to be moved.

Psalm 42:11 – Why are you cast down, O my soul, and why are you in turmoil within me? Hope in God; for I shall again praise him, my salvation and my God

Hebrews 4:16 – Let us then with confidence draw near to the throne of grace, that we may receive mercy and find grace to help in time of need.

Psalm 86:5 – For you, O Lord, are good and forgiving, abounding in steadfast love to all who call upon you.

Psalm 66:20 – Blessed be God, because he has not rejected my prayer or removed his steadfast love from me!

TRUST

Psalm 46:10 – Be still, and know that I am God. I will be exalted among the nations, I will be exalted in the earth!

Proverbs 3:5–6 – Trust in the Lord with all your heart, and do not lean on your own understanding. In all your ways acknowledge him, and he will make straight your paths.

Isaiah 41:10 – fear not, for I am with you; be not dismayed, for I am your God; I will strengthen you, I will help you, I will uphold you with my righteous right hand.

Isaiah 26:3 – You keep him in perfect peace whose mind is stayed on you, because he trusts in you.

Deuteronomy 31:6 – Be strong and courageous. Do not fear or be in dread of them, for it is the Lord your God who goes with you. He will not leave you or forsake you.

Psalm 62:1 – For God alone my soul waits in silence; from him comes my salvation.

Psalm 91:1–2 – He who dwells in the shelter of the Most High will abide in the shadow of the Almighty. I will say to the Lord, "My refuge and my fortress, my God, in whom I trust.

Hebrews 13:5 – Keep your life free from love of money, and be content with what you have, for he has said, "I will never leave you nor forsake you.

Isaiah 30:15 – For thus said the Lord God, the Holy One of Israel, "In returning and rest you shall be saved; in quietness and in trust shall be your strength." But you were unwilling

Colossians 2:6–7 – Therefore, as you received Christ Jesus the Lord, so walk in him, rooted and built up in him and established in the faith, just as you were taught, abounding in thanksgiving.

Isaiah 55:8–9 - For my thoughts are not your thoughts, neither are your ways my ways, declares the Lord. For as the heavens are higher than the earth, so are my ways higher than your ways and my thoughts than your thoughts.

HOPE

Romans 8:28 – And we know that for those who love God all things work together for good, for those who are called according to his purpose

Isaiah 40:31 – but they who wait for the Lord shall renew their strength; they shall mount up with wings like eagles; they shall run and not be weary; they shall walk and not faint.

Zephaniah 3:17 – The Lord your God is in your midst, a mighty one who will save; he will rejoice over you with gladness; he will quiet you by his love; he will exult over you with loud singing

Habakkuk 3:19 – God, the Lord, is my strength; he makes my feet like the deer's; he makes me tread on my high places.

Romans 15:13 – May the God of hope fill you with all joy and peace in believing, so that by the power of the Holy Spirit you may abound in hope.

1 Peter 1:3 – Blessed be the God and Father of our Lord Jesus Christ! According to his great mercy, he has caused us to be born again to a living hope through the resurrection of Jesus Christ from the dead,

Jeremiah 29:11 – For I know the plans I have for you, declares the Lord, plans for welfare and not for evil, to give you a future and a hope

Psalm 130:7 – O Israel, hope in the Lord! For with the Lord there is steadfast love, and with him is plentiful redemption.

Romans 8:38–39 – For I am sure that neither death nor life, nor angels nor rulers, nor things present nor things to come, nor powers, nor height nor depth, nor anything else in all creation, will be able to separate us from the love of God in Christ Jesus our Lord.

Jude 1:24 – Now to him who is able to keep you from stumbling and to present you blameless before the presence of his glory with great joy

Psalm 27:14 – Wait for the Lord; be strong, and let your heart take courage; wait for the Lord!

Romans 5:5 – and hope does not put us to shame, because God's love has been poured into our hearts through the Holy Spirit who has been given to us

JOY

Psalm 16:11 – You make known to me the path of life; in your presence there is fullness of joy; at your right hand are pleasures forevermore.

Psalm 23:1 – The Lord is my shepherd; I shall not want.

John 10:10 – The thief comes only to steal and kill and destroy. I came that they may have life and have it abundantly.

Philippians 4:6–7 – do not be anxious about anything, but in everything by prayer and supplication with thanksgiving let your requests be made known to God. And the peace of God, which surpasses all understanding, will guard your hearts and your minds in Christ Jesus.

Psalm 118:24 – This is the day that the Lord has made; let us rejoice and be glad in it.

1 Thessalonians 5:16–18 – Rejoice always, pray without ceasing, give thanks in all circumstances; for this is the will of God in Christ Jesus for you.

Psalm 37:4 – Delight yourself in the Lord, and he will give you the desires of your heart.

Psalm 145:18 – The Lord is near to all who call on him, to all who call on him in truth.

Nehemiah 8:10 – Then he said to them, "Go your way. Eat the fat and drink sweet wine and send portions to anyone who has nothing ready, for this day is holy to our Lord. And do not be grieved, for the joy of the Lord is your strength."

WISDOM

Psalm 119:105 – Your word is a lamp to my feet and a light to my path.

Micah 6:8 – He has told you, O man, what is good; and what does the Lord require of you but to do justice, and to love kindness, and to walk humbly with your God?

James 1:5 – If any of you lacks wisdom, let him ask God, who gives generously to all without reproach, and it will be given him.

Matthew 6:33 – But seek first the kingdom of God and his righteousness, and all these things will be added to you.

Proverbs 2:6 – For the Lord gives wisdom; from his mouth come knowledge and understanding

Proverbs 16:3 – Commit your work to the Lord, and your plans will be established.

Proverbs 16:9 – The heart of man plans his way, but the Lord establishes his steps.

James 1:17 – Every good gift and every perfect gift is from above, coming down from the Father of lights, with whom there is no variation or shadow due to change.

Romans 12:1–2 – I appeal to you therefore, brothers, by the mercies of God, to present your bodies as a living sacrifice, holy and acceptable to God, which is your spiritual worship. Do not be conformed to this world, but be transformed by the renewal of your mind, that by testing you may discern what is the will of God, what is good and acceptable and perfect.

Colossians 3:23 – Whatever you do, work heartily, as for the Lord and not for men

Hebrews 12:11 – For the moment all discipline seems painful rather than pleasant, but later it yields the peaceful fruit of righteousness to those who have been trained by it.

IDENTITY

Isaiah 43:1 – But now thus says the Lord, he who created you, O Jacob, he who formed you, O Israel: "Fear not, for I have redeemed you; I have called you by name, you are mine.

Psalm 139:13–14 – For you formed my inward parts; you knitted me together in my mother's womb. I praise you, for I am fearfully and wonderfully made. Wonderful are your works; my soul knows it very well.

Galatians 2:20 – I have been crucified with Christ. It is no longer I who live, but Christ who lives in me. And the life I now live in the flesh I live by faith in the Son of God, who loved me and gave himself for me.

Galatians 5:22–23 – But the fruit of the Spirit is love, joy, peace, patience, kindness, goodness, faithfulness, gentleness, self-control; against such things there is no law.

Colossians 3:3 – For you have died, and your life is hidden with Christ in God.

John 15:5 – I am the vine; you are the branches. Whoever abides in me and I in him, he it is that bears much fruit, for apart from me you can do nothing.

1 John 3:1 – See what kind of love the Father has given to us, that we should be called children of God; and so we are. The reason why the world does not know us is that it did not know him.

1 Peter 2:9 – But you are a chosen race, a royal priesthood, a holy nation, a people for his own possession, that you may proclaim the excellencies of him who called you out of darkness into his marvelous light.

Acts 17:28 – for "'In him we live and move and have our being'; as even some of your own poets have said, "'For we are indeed his offspring.'

2 Corinthians 4:16–18 – So we do not lose heart. Though our outer self is wasting away, our inner self is being renewed day by day. For this light momentary affliction is preparing for us an eternal weight of glory beyond all comparison, as we look not to the things that are seen but to the things that are unseen. For the things that are seen are transient, but the things that are unseen are eternal.

Psalm 73:26 – My flesh and my heart may fail, but God is the strength of my heart and my portion forever.

LOVE

1 John 4:19 – We love because he first loved us.

Matthew 22:37 – And he said to him, "You shall love the Lord your God with all your heart and with all your soul and with all your mind.

Luke 6:36 – Be merciful, even as your Father is merciful.

Ephesians 4:32 – Be kind to one another, tenderhearted, forgiving one another, as God in Christ forgave you.

Psalm 103:8 – The Lord is merciful and gracious, slow to anger and abounding in steadfast love.

John 6:35 – Jesus said to them, "I am the bread of life; whoever comes to me shall not hunger, and whoever believes in me shall never thirst.

Psalm 27:1 – The Lord is my light and my salvation; whom shall I fear? The Lord is the stronghold of my life; of whom shall I be afraid?

Psalm 121:1–2 – I lift up my eyes to the hills. From where does my help come? My help comes from the Lord, who made heaven and earth.

Romans 12:10 – Love one another with brotherly affection. Outdo one another in showing honor.

FAITH & COURAGE

Hebrews 11:1 – Now faith is the assurance of things hoped for, the conviction of things not seen.

Luke 1:37 – For nothing will be impossible with God."

Joshua 1:9 – Have I not commanded you? Be strong and courageous. Do not be frightened, and do not be dismayed, for the Lord your God is with you wherever you go."

Philippians 4:13 – I can do all things through him who strengthens me.

2 Timothy 1:7 – for God gave us a spirit not of fear but of power and love and self-control.

Matthew 28:20 – teaching them to observe all that I have commanded you. And behold, I am with you always, to the end of the age."

Ephesians 6:10 – Finally, be strong in the Lord and in the strength of his might.

Galatians 6:9 – And let us not grow weary of doing good, for in due season we will reap, if we do not give up.

Isaiah 49:15–16 – "Can a woman forget her nursing child, that she should have no compassion on the son of her womb? Even these may forget, yet I will not forget you. Behold, I have engraved you on the palms of my hands; your walls are continually before me

1 Corinthians 16:13–14 – Be watchful, stand firm in the faith, act like men, be strong. Let all that you do be done in love.

PERSEVERANCE & GROWTH

Philippians 1:6 – And I am sure of this, that he who began a good work in you will bring it to completion at the day of Jesus Christ.

Philippians 2:13 – for it is God who works in you, both to will and to work for his good pleasure.

1 Corinthians 10:13 – No temptation has overtaken you that is not common to man. God is faithful, and he will not let you be tempted beyond your ability, but with the temptation he will also provide the way of escape, that you may be able to endure it.

1 Corinthians 1:9 – God is faithful, by whom you were called into the fellowship of his Son, Jesus Christ our Lord.

Psalm 51:10 – Create in me a clean heart, O God, and renew a right spirit within me.

2 Corinthians 12:9 – But he said to me, "My grace is sufficient for you, for my power is made perfect in weakness." Therefore, I will

boast all the more gladly of my weaknesses, so that the power of Christ may rest upon me.

James 1:2–4 – Count it all joy, my brothers, when you meet trials of various kinds, for you know that the testing of your faith produces steadfastness. And let steadfastness have its full effect, that you may be perfect and complete, lacking in nothing.

The Lord bless you and keep you; the Lord make his face to shine upon you and be gracious to you; the Lord lift up his countenance upon you and give you peace.

Numbers 6:24-26